Whitfield
404-843-

The Yoga of Marijuana

By

Joan M. Bello, M.S.

***

Lifeservices Press, Inc.
Susquehanna, PA 18847

The Yoga of Marijuana

Copyright 2015

All rights reserved.

No part of this book may be reproduced in any manner whatsoever without permission from the publisher except for brief quotes in critical articles or reviews.

Cover image of the Marijuana leaf is not to be used in anyway without the express permission from the artist. Copyrighted by Tanya Bucel.

Published by LIFESERVICES PRESS, INC.
POST OFFICE BOX 61
SUSQUEHANNA, PENNSYLVANIA 18465

www.benefitsofmarijuana.com

First Edition
Library of Congress Catalogue Card Number:
ISBN-13: 978-1466357457
ISBN-10: 1466357452
Printed in the U.S.A.

ACKNOWLEDGMENT

Cultural Narcissism of Western Civilization
Venerates
Hedonistic Material Technology
Fosters
Alienation from Age-Old Tradition
And
Timeless Human Values
Ergo
A Collective, Unconscious Yearning Exists
Summoning
Abandoned, Innate Higher Ideals
Reflecting
Compassion and Humility
Hence
The Clarion Call Exists
For
The Marijuana Consciousness!

Special Appreciation:

To Tanya Bucel, my daughter-in-law for the cover design which involved even gilding the marijuana leaf for its photo; for her proficiency in formatting the entire text; and most especially for the generous lending of her time with such patient diligence.

To Barbra Haynes, my daughter, for her editing: I must express great gratitude for her attentiveness to each detail and her thoughtful consideration of every subject, always letting me know when there was yet more work to be done.

To Nicholas R. Haynes, my teenage grandson for his technical talents: When all else failed, his computer skills, quite effortlessly permitted my vision to become a reality. Thank you, Nicholas, I am impressed!

And to my lifelong friend and sister activist, Kay Lee, who added the finishing touches through her unique perception to appreciate what is most significant, I am ever indebted for her help and her friendship.

Lead Us from Unreal to Real
Lead Us from Darkness to Light
Lead Us from the Fear of Death
To Knowledge of Immortality
Om, Shanti, Shanti, Shanti

DEDICATION & TRIBUTE

MAIDENS FAIR - Fragile Faces Toward The One
FRAGRANT FLAVOR of Graceful Way
SPIRITED SILHOUETS - Emerald Skirts Beneath The Sun
MUSE OF MARIJUANA – Messenger for Modern Day

PLANT OF KNOWLEDGE – Mysterious and Pure
FERTILE FEMALES – Full with Flower
HEALING HANDS – Outstretched To Cure
PERENNIAL PEACE – Potent with Power

FROM YOUR GRACEFUL FERNLIKE LEAVES
TURNED GOLDEN FROM THE LIGHT
FOR EVERY SEEKER WHO RECEIVES
IS THE BLESSING OF CLEAR SIGHT

THE WORLD HAS IDOLS ONCE AGAIN
TO MAKE UP FOR THE LACK OF LOVE
BUT EMPTY PLEASURE BECOMES JUST PAIN
SUFFERING FITS THIS BLACKENED DOVE

FAME, FORTUNE, MONEY ARE IN ESTEEM
IN THIS MODERN AGE OF MIND
FAITH, HOPE, LOVE – JUST A DREAM
WE NO LONGER TRY TO FIND

THERE IS MORE – IF WE JUST LOOK
TURN THE COVER – READ THE BOOK
THE FLOWER FEARED MAKES REAL TO SEE
THE CAUSES FOR OUR MISERY

IN THE BOOKS OF OLD
WRIT FOR ANY DAY
WHEN THE HEART IS COLD
HELP IS ON THE WAY

ALWAYS CLOAKED IN SOME DISGUISE
AND HIDDEN BY DUPLICITY
NOT APPEARING AS A PRIZE
COSTUMED IN SIMPLICITY

KNOW YOURSELF, SAID ALL THE SEERS
DON'T DENY THE PAIN OF TEARS
LIVE, BE FULL, BE UNAFRAID
LOOK WITHIN TO WHY YOU'RE MADE

MYSTERIOUS MOTHER OF ETERNITY
ETHEREAL FATHER OF INFINITY
YOU'VE SENT THE MESSAGE AS A FLOWER
FULL OF PEACE AND LOVE AND POWER

THEY'VE RULED IT OUT
AND CALLED IT WEED
THEY'RE FULL OF DOUBT
AND FULL OF NEED

BUT I BELONG TO THE INVISIBLE STREAMING
COURSING FOREVER WITH HOLY MEANING
THERE'S NO ESCAPING THE ETERNAL GOAL
IT'S IN MY BLOOD AND HEART AND SOUL

THO I PUZZLE OVER WHAT I SEE
WHEN I'M WITHOUT THE KNOWLEDGE TREE
I'VE LEARNED MY LESSON IN A PERFUMED ROOM
I'VE SEEN THE COLOR IN THE PLUME

I KNOW THE WEAVER OF THE LOOM
I AM THE KEEPER OF THE KEY
AS IT WAS
IT WILL ALWAYS BE

Table of Contents

SPECIAL APPRECIATION: 8

CAN I TALK TO YOU AND YOU TO ME? 19
    WHAT IS THE MARIJUANA CONSCIOUSNESS? 19

INTRODUCTION 29
    MARIJUANA CONSCIOUSNESS - INTUITIVE HEALTH 30
    MARIJUANA: AN INTUITIVE SURVIVAL RESPONSE 31
    COUNTER CULTURE IS SUSPECT BY THE MAINSTREAM 31
    THE ESSENTIAL FEAR OF MARIJUANA 32
    MARIJUANA THREATENS COMPETITIVE VALUES 32
    TURNING FROM THE OUTER TO THE INNER 33
    AWAKENING TO AN ALTERED REALITY BY MARIJUANA 34

TIMELESS CONNECTION OF 35

YOGA WITH MARIJUANA 35
    THE OBJECTIVE OF YOGA 35
    THE YOGA SUTRAS 36
    THE YOGA OF MARIJUANA 38
    MARIJUANA - THE ACCELERATOR 40
    MANIFESTATIONS OF THE MASTER TEACHER: THE GURU 40
    MIND FIELD: DEFINED 41

THE SUTRAS 43
    "YOGA IS CESSATION OF THE MODIFICATIONS OF THE MIND FIELD" 43
    THE LAKE 44
    THE SCIENCE OF CANNABIS AND PAUSING THE MIND 46
    PRACTICE OF YOGA / EFFECTS OF MARIJUANA 47
    MEDITATION AND PAUSING THOUGHT 47
    THE BREATH 48
    ENCULTURATION MEANS THAT THE CULTURE IS IN US! 51
    THE PEOPLE FOUND THE WAY: 53
    THE LEGEND OF THE ORIGIN OF MARIJUANA 53
    HEALTH, SPIRITUAL RIPENING, INTEREST AND INTENTIONALITY 55

FEATURES OF YOGA AND HISTORY OF MARIJUANA 58
    THE MARIJUANA CONSCIOUSNESS PREDATES THE SCIENCE OF YOGA 59
    THE LOST AND FOUND CITY OF HARAPPAN 60
    THE YUGAS OF EASTERN METAPHYSICS 61
    A POPULAR HINDU TALE TO BOGGLE THE IMAGINATION 61
    THE BRIDGE BEFORE HISTORY (NAMED ADAM'S BRIDGE) 62

THE PERPETUAL SEARCH	64
MOMENTS IN HISTORY THAT MATTER	65
YOGA OF MARIJUANA: COLLECTIVE TURNING TOWARD THE ESSENTIAL	65
THE PAUSE IS THE DOORWAY TO INTELLIGENCE	66

CANNABIS SATIVA: SCIENCE AND THE PLANT ... 67

THE INTERFACE OF CANNABIS SATIVA WITH THE HUMAN ORGANISM:	68
THE CANNABIS SYSTEM	68
WHY IS THE CANNABIS SATIVA PLANT SO OVERWHELMINGLY HELPFUL TO THE HUMAN ORGANISM?	69
GENERAL BENEFITS OF MARIJUANA	70
DUALISM OF BODY AND MIND	72
RESOLVING THE OPPOSITES	74
COMPATIBLE GIFT OF MARIJUANA	76

RELIGION VS. THE MARIJUANA CONSCIOUSNESS ... 77

ADAM KADMON – (KABBALAH MAN)	78
OBJECTIVE WITNESS	79

IDENTIFICATION DISSOLVES WITH MARIJUANA ... 79

MATERIALISM DOES NOT SATISFY THE SPIRIT	80
PRESENT POTENTIAL FOR GROWTH IS MAGNIFIED TODAY	80
IMBALANCE MAINTAINS THE CULTURE	82
WHO IS INTERESTED AND WHY IS UNDECIPHERABLE	82
THE INNER HUMAN MAKE-UP PREVAILS	83
MATERIALISM GIVING BIRTH TO SPIRITUAL RESURGENCE	84
EASTERN UNDERSTANDING REINVIGORATED	84
INDIA DOES NOT DENY ITS HERITAGE	85
FROM WHENCE HAS COME THIS WISDOM	85
THE DEPTH OF INDIAN PHILOSOPHY	86
THE UNIVERSAL REALISM OF INDIAN PHILOSOPHY	86
INDIAN ESOTERIC UNDERSTANDING	86
INDIA OF OLD	88
YOGA: HIDDEN ROOTS AND MODERN RELEVANCE	88
YOGA OF MARIJUANA VS. CLASSICAL YOGA	90

SUMMING UP ... 90

AUTHOR'S AFTERWORD ... 93

BIBLIOGRAPHY ... 101

INDEX ... 105

The Yoga of Marijuana

The First of Three Parts

FROM THE AUTHOR

This presentation will explain the enhancement toward the uncovering of consciousness that is not only a possibility through the Yoga of Marijuana but is, in fact, an ongoing, although little known, abiding reality. In addition, the work will clarify how Marijuana serves as proactive and perennial guide on the Path to Enlightenment as reflected in and precedent to Classical Yoga as it comes down to us from the primordial and hidden Tantra.

*Enlightenment Recognizes Everything as
Interconnected and Interdependent.
It is absence of self concern and absolute attentiveness.
According to all Esoteric Disciplines,
Enlightenment is the Highest Evolution.
Enlightenment is Full Transformation of Heart and Mind
Expressed in Compassionate Detachment.
Enlightenment is a state of Permanent Bliss,
Infinite Compassion, Full Awareness and Pure Wisdom.
It is Not an Achievement
But Realization of What Is.*
(Lao Tzu)

*Separation IS the Ultimate Altered State of Consciousness.
Enlightenment is Not an Altered State of Consciousness.
Enlightenment is an **Un-Altered** State of Consciousness.
It is Pure Consciousness - As It Actually IS
Before having been Altered in any Way.*
(Adyashanti)

CAN I TALK TO YOU AND YOU TO ME?

What is the Marijuana Consciousness?

How Does it Change a Person? Who Can Understand It?

There are states of being that are beyond words. But if one is addressing a particular event, experience, knowledge, intuitive sense, etc. that has been shared, is part and parcel of the understanding of both of us (reader and writer), then there can surely be words that trigger the ineffable remembrance. Such is the case with the discussion at hand. If you have tasted the orange, then describing its sweet astringency that is both velvet and tangy, whose fruit is hard yet soft and stringy yet silky will make sense and we can commiserate. But if you have not tasted the orange, you will not garner the experience from any description. You do not have the convolutions in your brain or the impressions in your mind for recognition.

Likewise, in describing The Marijuana Consciousness, if your memory banks did not make the entry in the first place, this presentation is just an exercise in intellectual thought, with nothing whatsoever to do with a mutual sense of distant déjà vu that is scarcely, if ever, spoken to and which is absolutely inherently part and parcel of the mystery of this Ancient Earth Teacher. It is an event of profound wonder escorted by a resounding cosmic silence that is stunningly most noticeable as a novice in the early stages of The Marijuana Effect. <u>It is being vividly awake in/to/of the present moment where the energy is recognized to be of a finer quality than usual.</u>

The State of Mind Evoked by Marijuana has a Vibrational Resonance that is Recognized by Many as an Unmistakable Attuning to an Invisible yet Palpably Familiar Lost Reality that some (of us) find Magnetic.
(Bello)

The Marijuana Experience is a whole person realization that is deemed to be the way it should be! Or the way it once was! And the way it can be again. There is depth and meaning and a bit more to all existence that is both otherworldly yet safe. Among those who share in the soul-felt communion of The Marijuana Consciousness, there is an indescribable kinship. Self-knowledge and liberation from personal identification, along with courage, compassion and serenity are intrinsic to the Promise of Marijuana for those for whom growth toward the spirit is an intentional and purposefully chosen path.

There is historical evidence of regular spiritual practice with Marijuana some 20,000 years ago. No verification further back exists, simply because no objective proof of human habits goes back further. According to the science of antiquity, Cannabis Sativa and our ancestors co-habited in persistent close community as a mutually beneficial outcome of life on Earth, although The Plant of Many Uses predates our specie by hundreds of millions of years.

*It was Here Before Us;
Was Here For Us
Is Attuned To Us
And has Always Been Incorporated
By Us in All Our Many Endeavors.*

There are certain signposts that stand out in the records of civilization when there was a collective synchrony of one pointed focus toward the next step of evolution. Such visible eruptions in times past were culminations of dissatisfaction among receptive groups of people inspired by the possibility of apprehending more than just the surface of existence. The River of Consciousness travels throughout the entire gamut of unconscious civilization since the dualism of manifestation is necessarily expressed in contrasts and polarities. Wherever there is a dominant force, there exists opposition. Where there is darkness, the light is bound to shine. The Buddha, Siva, and Christ were messengers of hope born from their tumultuous and hopeless times. They spoke to the usually ignored Higher Energy Centers which are in perfect harmony with the Marijuana Experience.

This presentation seeks to shed light on the impact of the ancient Cannabis Sativa as it catalyzes intentional and intentionally intense methods to rise from the self-serving divisive concerns of ordinary existence to the stunning realization of the Oneness of All. How Marijuana has emerged onto the world stage to be integrated into vastly dissimilar segments throughout the Dominant Culture despite strong and long standing opposition is a natural consequence of the materialistic lifestyle that summons an ageless, profound and unquenchable collective human need for meaning. Throughout the unending periods of social confusion, the perennial affinity for Marijuana persists. For those who would gather wisdom, the timeless knowledge to be gleaned from the Spirit within The Flower is the perpetual candle in the darkness of ignorance.

Over the course of an individual life term on the planet, a regularity of experience with Marijuana creates a gentle friction between what is authentic and what has been internalized. Continuous awareness of the schism serves as <u>a catalyst toward transforming the personality</u> which can include feelings of paranoia especially in the beginning of the journey when delusion and defense mechanisms are necessarily and painfully stripped away.

Although by no means acknowledged but instead actually definitely hidden over the past centuries of materialistic principles, The Yoga of Marijuana is and has always been a forward moving, Unbroken Tradition of the marriage between the primordial Cannabis Sativa Plant and the Science of Yoga. This is esoteric knowledge that is being brought to the light of the civilization as it always is in times of potential transformation.

The Tradition of Marijuana will not be served by a superficial exposition. Whereas answers to the deepest questions are not found by searching but are instead exposed in stillness, alteration to a higher sustained consciousness is not only born of an uplifting experience but mandates also a serious aspiration by the seeker.

It is the aim of this introductory work to spark the interest of those for whom the Marijuana Consciousness is of utmost importance and to prepare the way for recognition and reception of <u>The Yoga of Marijuana.</u>

(About The Author)
Credentials and Motivation of this Author

By formal measure, I have the credentials to speak to Yoga Science and to the effects and Experience of Marijuana. I have a Master's Degree in Eastern Studies and Holistic Health; have been a lifelong student of Yoga; and studied Sanskrit for seven years intending to translate the ancient hidden wisdom having to do with the sacred herb. I never became proficient enough to fulfill that objective but I am extremely well-versed in the subject.

I am 72 years old, in good health, of sound mind and of passionate heart when it comes to the connection between Yoga Science and the consciousness evoked by Marijuana. My experience with this maligned plant spans more than half my lifetime, having become a devotee before I was 30 years old. My research about Marijuana has likewise been an unending endeavor of over forty years. My expectations concerning The Benefits of Marijuana have far exceeded even my ideals as proven by the most recent research to the point that I no longer harbor any restrictions whatsoever for the helpful, healthful and mystical possibilities inherent in this mysterious vegetable for all things manifest.

Two conditions validate my devotion and trust in the Guiding Force within The Sativa. First and foremost, I am not alone. I stand in the presence of an enduring kindred understanding that is not limited to either era or locale. The Marijuana Community is an ongoing group of followers, firmly planted in mainstream history and in the earliest records of our specie.

United by common knowledge, supported by each other, we persevere. Throughout the annals of time, however understated, The Marijuana Community has withstood intimidation and repression with an enduring spiritual integrity. To uncover The Marijuana Path gives glorious substantiation to our deepest suspicions. While it has often been concealed, it has never been diminished. What so many of us have sensed in the core of our being is finally fortified by the knowledge of our shared and righteous struggle. It is humbling yet immensely exhilarating to know the truth of how long our tradition has endured.

Secondly, I have personally been granted an intuitive and far ranging definitive and life-changing insight into the esoteric meaning of Marijuana as a universal medium for human evolution. And I am not alone in this realization. Intuition does not form convolutions in the brain. It is not remembrance of an embodied occurrence. In fact, the seeing in-tu-it does not require any empirical knowledge of the subject at hand. It is actually beyond physical experience, rational interpretation and/or deductive reasoning. It cannot be explained for it is beyond language and thought. It is re-cognition of what one knows from an essential but non-physical realm of being that can be sensed but not seen on the material plane of existence.

Those of Us Who Share
In The Yoga of Marijuana
Travel Together
Toward That to which We are Irresistibly Drawn,
Gaining Strength from the Fact
That We Are Not Alone.

It seems thus:
In some other time far removed from the present, in a space of mind so very unfamiliar from the ordinary and exceedingly different from what is my usual mode, in an unrecognizable place, from a distance that I cannot quite assess clearly as great or small, that appears not as vivid as a memory yet not as murky as a dream, a very long time ago or perhaps in some future era extending into an other-worldly dimension, I envision myself, as in an old and worn photograph, wearing faded yet obviously comfortable familiar attire, within a shadowed silent enclosure, holding a timeworn tome that is unmistakably heavy but nevertheless has an apparent paradoxical weightlessness and blinding radiance suggestive of secret knowledge that I cannot Quite decipher but that I am trying desperately to fathom from the depths of my being.

In a vivid, unforgettable image, there in a fleeting moment of recognition as the cloud of confusion dissipates ever so mercifully, the barely legible words come into focus: Oshadhi: The Yoga of Herbs.

Such is the permanent, haunting picture embedded in my mind or my soul or my memory. It speaks to me. It commands that I remember that which I have been privileged to understand but that I have somehow nearly lost through the intricacies of the mystery. So it is written or so it seems that just as a scribe faithfully copies from the inspired book that I am so charged to retrace the forgotten wisdom for those on this eternal trek to Higher Consciousness.

Such is the impetus for this author in transliterating the timeless revelation of The Yoga of Marijuana.

Note:

The whole of this work is envisioned as all of a piece. It is to give those for whom Marijuana is The Perennial Teacher a lucid picture of spiritual fulfillment, including also its implementation through The Marijuana Consciousness. It is presented here, however in three parts owing, First of All, to the limitations of this author to explain such a grand theme, and Secondly, in deference to the linear mindset of the modern reader. The hope is for the three sequential parts to coalesce over time in both the cognitive and intuitional faculties and be internalized holographically as a unified reality.

The Yoga of Marijuana is the First Part of The Trilogy. It presents the basic philosophical and historical underpinnings of *Yoga Science*, with its intentionally hidden, ancient and originating connection to *The Yoga of Marijuana*; the palpable synchronicity between these two paths which has always been ardently denied by the established religions and traditions, as well as the reasons for the strong resistance; and, how and why the primordial Practice of Marijuana as an esoteric discipline is re-emerging, with such power at this moment in time in this materialistic period of civilization

The Yoga of Marijuana is being uncovered as an uninterrupted, ancient, secreted and independent *Way to Enlightenment* for those who resonate with this path and are prepared to resume their *journey* to self-realization from some previous time, state or embodiment.

The Tantra of Marijuana is Part II and while it is written, it is not yet polished enough to present to the readership.

Marijuana and Yoga Practice (Section III) covers the practices of Yoga Science; the specifics of their benefits; the interface of *The Marijuana Consciousness* with Yogic Philosophy; and the effects of Marijuana as the originating force behind Yoga.

INTRODUCTION

Medical marijuana is here to stay. Its future is assured with the astoundingly positive results of science, the incessant testimony of so many grateful patients and the steadfast determination of all activists worldwide. But when it comes to evolving beyond the state of ego-centeredness, the *Benefits of The Marijuana Consciousness* are not appreciated. Aspiring to a state of inner wisdom is not even a mainstream goal. In practical life, the intrinsic yearning for understanding the significance of existence is lost among infinite distractions and all things spiritual are disparaged.

In contrast, those of us who invite *The Marijuana Consciousness* regularly welcome the expanded appreciation of authenticity that it imparts. While it is true that the interests and motives of the *Marijuana Way of Life* are different from the norm, it is not *Marijuana* that turns us away from the material goals of the culture but their inability to satisfy the essence of our being. Perhaps we are that fringe of society that most desires freedom, although it does not seem that way since millions of us have been imprisoned for our *Marijuana Practice*.

Rather than physical or social restriction, however, the lack of freedom in our own minds, the inability to express who we are, what we feel and where our allegiance lay loom large as unbearable restrictions that we need very much to shed. An encoded rhythm within our private lives that is and always was out of sync with the tempo of the outer world is exposed as well as embraced with the internal recognition of the consciousness evoked by Marijuana. "Stoned thinking," coined years ago by Dr. Andrew Weil, is liberation from external taming. It is always toward tolerance and cooperation rather than exclusion and competition. Such freedom from the bonds of social conditioning, quite naturally engenders suspicion and fear in the established regimentation.

29

When influenced by *The Marijuana Consciousness*, an unbiased perspective of timeless principles emerges which inherently contradicts the malleability of a homogenous citizenry. That we should all think the same, want the same, and so oil the mechanical work wheels with great competitive herd-like productive sameness stands for survival for the major culture. With ever more sophisticated (methods of) conditioning, the collective psyche of the community is filled with never-ending desire that guarantees continuation of the status quo. The cycle of discontent is a mechanical, self-propelling process without malicious intent but fueled instead by fear borne of ignorance. The promise of security remains in the future with the individual focus on winning the prize. Regardless of the reward, it is not enough for *members of the Marijuana World* who harbor an unquenchable *inner* thirst for essential values of compassion, trust and knowledge that although intangible nevertheless are of utmost significance for us in our recurring journey toward reality.

Marijuana Consciousness - Intuitive Health

It is no coincidence that as our culture fast forwards to a life less-measured and more unconscious that many are finding respite from the fast-paced and superficial daily fare through the fuller awareness of *The Marijuana Consciousness*. As a coping mechanism that serves psychological and physical health, Marijuana is eminently safe, effective and illegally used by (hundreds of) millions of citizens worldwide. While research of Cannabis as a remedy for all manner of disease demonstrates astonishingly favorable outcomes, the fact that this ubiquitous Earth Medicine features an uncanny ability to balance automatic integration of body, mind and *Breath* is unsuspected,* the significance of which is beyond imagination. *Likewise,* when it comes to the sense of well-being and the experience of Higher Consciousness, the essential implication of regularity in *the Pattern of the Breath* is lost to the objectivity of technological medicine. ** See "The Breath," Page 48*

Marijuana: An Intuitive Survival Response

In light of the therapeutic effects of this prehistoric plant, we can theorize that the unswerving and constantly escalating world-wide collective magnetic attraction to the Marijuana Experience is an *intuitive* (albeit involuntary) *survival response to the imbalance of modern civilization*. We can do this having studied Marijuana with its benefits for the human organism through a simultaneous relaxing and stimulating, delicate and indeed utterly unique life-enhancing process of increased *whole being* oxygenation of clinically proven but yet to be understood, *balancing, modulating and moderating rewards*. (IOM)

Counter Culture is Suspect by the Mainstream

Although the spiritual (vibrational) effect that attracts so many to Marijuana has gone unrecognized, yet it is, in fact instinctively resisted. *States of fuller awareness* have no place in objective science. There is no interest or appreciation of the interface between physical health and higher planes of being. Even addressing advanced mental modes is suspect in the material mindset. But within the society, there is a growing minority who sense the spiritual void of continuous diversion, conformity and unbridled attainment of status, power or thrills. The ***rebellious underground*** is actually a recurring theme throughout the recording of all civilizations. Those who hear a different calling naturally respond to the dimension of human life that, although unseen is of supreme importance.

There is always the Culture and That which runs Counter to It.
Down through the Annals of Time,
There is an Endless Streaming of Conscious Seekers,
Coursing within the Dominant World,
Who Perceive a More Expansive Way of Living and Being.
It Cannot Be Repressed.
The Drive to Higher Consciousness and all Paths to It Cannot Be Stamped Out. It is a Continuous and Constant Re-emergent Theme of The Human Race. (Bello)

The Essential Fear of Marijuana

Juice/Oil/Vapors/Cannabis *Medibles*, Hemp fields and now legalized Marijuana have gained a foothold in the progressive, youth driven arenas. The *Politics of Marijuana* is being fueled by the promise of monetary gain and determined, disgruntled voters. Meanwhile, the major culture is gravely threatened by the clarity evoked by the plant that is automatically accessed and nearly effortlessly integrated with the *intentional invitation to alter consciousness*. Although obviously not every participant in the Cannabis Culture is interested in spiritual growth, nevertheless everyone who willingly and enthusiastically partakes of the Majestic Flower of Peace regularly enhances their personal comprehension of community and humanity.

The exclusivity principle of striving solely for oneself without notice or concern for the fate of the *other* is incompatible with the *Marijuana Way of Thinking and Breathing*. Psychologically speaking, Marijuana fosters the higher emotions of caring, sharing and tolerance. There is less emphasis placed on personal acquisition and achievement and more on inner understanding and righteousness. Competition is eased out and recognized as an inhumane ethic, especially in these dire times when the need for compassion is so obvious.

Marijuana Threatens Competitive Values

Impact of this mind-expanding plant connects us to the earth, all its creatures and our essential selves. Even the way that Marijuana molecules inform the body displays a sophisticated, intuitive cooperation that is both understated and holistic. But the *materialistic ethic* runs on a separatist mentality and is weakened by anything that encourages cooperating rather than competing. Taking time to smell the roses or share their loveliness does not bode well for a society built on primitive principles and upheld by perverse practices. The camaraderie that often unfolds with Marijuana endangers the fundamental structure of capitalism and all forms of social containment.

While *The Marijuana Consciousness* changes how you view the world, yourself and relationships, the makeover in perception and perspective is far from being easily discerned by outside observers. The undetectable shift in the way a person thinks and feels is predictably and inevitably met with mistrust by the greater community. Being a certain gender, race or even ethnicity or being drunk or depressed can be identified. But internal attitudes, thoughts and plans of the *Marijuana Devotee* are easily concealed, leaving the insecure, suspicious majority in the dark, wondering who is thinking straight and who is outside the proscribed mode. (Ergo: Urinalysis)

Turning From the Outer to the Inner

But there need not be any confusion whatsoever. Regardless of the lack of visible signposts and despite denial by those who are stigmatized, intimidated, persecuted and prosecuted by/for their loyalty to consciousness brought about through Marijuana, **Be Absolutely Assured** that regular and deliberate *Practice of Marijuana* (not *medica*l) is unquestionably, although conceivably an unconscious and moreover often understated, *purposeful turning away from* the social values of accumulation, status, productivity and power toward the *esoteric* or from *the seen to the unseen*. Without a doubt, this outcome is rightly feared by the established structure since it can be understood as *holding-in-the-highest-esteem something other and exceedingly more worthy* than the cultural ambition. The point of view imparted by *The Marijuana Consciousness* is compatible with serenity, stillness, tolerance, acceptance and kindness which sadly pits it against the popular gods of capitalism and competition and the incessant worldly distractions.

> *The Danger of Psychedelic Drugs,*
> *The Danger of Mind-Opening*
> *…Of Consciousness Expansion,*
> *The Danger of Inner Discovery*
> *Is a Danger to The Establishment.* (Leary)

Awakening to an Altered Reality by Marijuana

The first Marijuana Experience can be startling. Awakening to an utterly different reality from what is usual but nevertheless strangely familiar is a *whole person* relaxation that engenders noticing and perceiving with more depth. Over a period of time, the condition evoked by Marijuana lends a sense of ease that has been described by many as feeling "normal." Whether a refreshed interpretation of the glory of existence or practically speaking, just the release of defense mechanisms, Marijuana increases both intensity and vitality by transferring refined energy from plant to subject.

In the long-standing cultures of the world, healing by herbs was (and still is) realized as a physical, mental and spiritual harmonizing of the accumulation of cosmic forces that comprise the unique energetic signature of the organism. But the modern material mindset is far removed from such an understanding. Instead our medicines and techniques for healing are based only on the gross manifestations of forces without taking into consideration their source. Of course, intellectually we know that all life is totally dependent on the sun, yet we have lost our reverence for what that means. We are no longer in communion with the essence of life.

> *Plants Transmit the Vital-Emotional Impulses,*
> *The Life Force that is Hidden in Light.*
> *That is the Gift, the Grace, the Power of Plants*
>
> *...Plants bring the Nourishing Power of the Sun.*
> *Plants exist to Transmute Light into Life.*
> *Humans exist to Transmute Life into Consciousness*
>
> *...Plants Transmute Light into Life*
> *Through Photosynthesis.*
> *Humans Transmute Life into Consciousness*
> *Through Perception.* (Frawley & Lad)

TIMELESS CONNECTION OF YOGA WITH MARIJUANA

The Objective of Yoga

The system of Classical Yoga is older than recorded history. It is experiential and experimental in that every seeker must ultimately and independently find the truth. Yogic methods are very exacting. They are based in intuition yet implemented by a precise yet extremely pragmatic science that keys into the furthest possibility of human evolution. Yoga is a time-worn scheme for reworking psychological and physical habits that hinder our perception of the *whole* (of existence). It is logically geared toward a relaxed mind to offset the frenzied striving of materialism. Its disciplines are demanding and require strong motivation, as well as an ordered lifestyle. Yoga requires the ability to focus. It will not accommodate to the culturally encouraged short attention span of the majority. It is a rare bird, indeed who carries out the Yogic disciplines with utmost diligence while maintaining the humility of a true aspirant. For these reasons, the *Yoga Movement* attracts relatively few serious practitioners. No noticeable alteration in a student's acting or thinking takes place. Therefore, Yoga is not in any way viewed as a threat to the status quo as is Marijuana. In addition, the message of Yoga Science has been diluted by the mammoth capitalist machine to accommodate modern society.

When Traditional Yoga reached our Western Shores
… It was gradually stripped of its
Spiritual Orientation and Remodeled into Fitness Training.
(Feuerstein)

But the Science of Yoga is an Enduring Path.
Its Essence is Mysterious and Patient.
Its Wisdom Embraces all Contingencies.
It Anticipates that Students May Require Scores of Terms
Through Various Eras, on the Journey to Ultimate Knowledge. (Bello)

Note:
Reincarnation is fundamental to the doctrine of Yoga Science; and it was also central to Western esoteric thought until it was purposely erased by the Catholic Church (14th Century), which promised instead life eternal by devotion, service and donations of wealth to *The Holy Mother Church*. To be clear, reincarnation is not resurrection of the person. It does not therefore serve as escape to the dread of dying; it is simply recognition that energy is not destroyed, just transformed.
(*Recurrence vs. Reincarnation,* Appendix I)

The Yoga Sutras

The ultimate authority for every student of Yoga Science is the ancient Indian tome of lessons, referred to as The Yoga Sutras. In all, there are 196 sutras (*aphorisms*), originally designed to be memorized which explains why they are in such very cryptic form. Numerous and scholarly volumes of explanatory commentaries have been written over many, many centuries, by hundreds of scholars around the world, attempting to encapsulate the whole of the esoteric message in order to help diligent students uncover the often veiled meaning of each lesson. Patanjali is the sage who is credited with setting down the Sutras in an ordered and written form. But for a very long time, before Patanjali came on the scene, *The Sutras* were held in the highest regard by the sages and the people alike, although the teaching was imparted exclusively to worthy veteran practitioners as they sat at the foot of a Master Yogi.

The Yoga Sutras speaks to the unknown potential that exists *beyond the mind*; it teaches that such a state is accessible to anyone who manages to shed every shred of countless past lifetimes of emotional baggage which is not only accepted but expected to take countless life terms. The main thought that runs through every thread of The Sutras is that eternal bliss awaits us all, sooner or later if we just realize it, thus the term *self-realization* - which is the cause and purpose of human life.

According to <u>The Sutras,</u> there are five paths to *self-realization:*
1) **Meditation** (*Concentrated Mind*): fits with peaceful eras;
2) **Oshadhi (Herbs/Plants/Elixirs): suitable for chaotic times and the main focus of this presentation.**
3) **Mantra** (*Repetitive Sound*): Useful to drown out trivia;
4) **Sacrifice** (*Labors of Love*): Appropriate in virtuous times;
5) **Birth:** (*Supreme Consciousness):* Mysteriously manifest in a Visibly Recognizable Guide frequently in the Darkest Ages.

While Meditation, Selfless-Service and Mantra are self-explanatory, <u>Enlightenment by Birth</u> addresses an extraordinary happening: If some have attained enlightenment apparently without effort, we must assume that they prepared for that auspicious moment over many lifetimes. Without the notion of rebirth…we are left with only one other explanation, namely that their enlightenment was simply a random occurrence. (They lucked out.) If we accept this, we have to assume that spiritual effort is a waste of time - live as we will and hope for the best. (What most people have opted to do). Instead of being free, they suffer from much unhappiness.)
(Feuerstein)

The Way of Herbs is mentioned only in the original list, with no details. It is noticeably absent in most commentaries. *Oshadhi* is surely not insignificant as one of **only Five Ways** to ultimate wisdom. Then why is this major method so clearly neglected? (*In <u>The Tantra of Marijuana</u>, Part II, this omission is discussed, but simply stated: political agendas always existed.*) Being deliberately ignored, The Path of Oshadhi has no map, system or planned practice. Intuition is the only Guide, which allows for great Freedom, as well as the grave risk of losing one's way.

(In Sanskrit), *The Plant, Osadhi is Receptacle or Mind (DHI) in which there is burning transformation (OSA) …The Human Being is The Plant of Consciousness …The Plant feeds our Minds and Nervous System. As Above, So Below. All the Universe is a Metamorphosis of Light.*
(Frawley & Lad)

Oshadhis, The Way of Herbs is a non-linear, individualized and independent Conduit to Enlightenment, wherein clerics are superfluous. This offers a logical reason why *The Way of Herbs* was/is disregarded by both establishment and commentators. Without an interpretative explanation by the sages, those who tread the Path of Oshadhi are left to fend for themselves in deciding what practices to follow. They stand apart from the mapped out, safer journey to ultimate knowledge since there is no External Guidance, such as a Guru. There is just the Inner *Voice of Intuition*, often awakened by the Spirit within *The Flower of Consciousness*.

Oshadhis suggests multiple Entheogens as companions and as aides to Transcendence. Yet the bounteous growth of Bhangi throughout the tropical land; its adoration in ancient texts; the lack of serious references in scripture regarding other Plant Teachers; while knowing that the High Priests rejected autonomous study (and were in charge) and therefore probably censored much that was recorded, it is logical, verifiable and intuitive to accept that *The Yoga of Herbs* speaks to Bhangi, that which *gives life and joy* to the partaker.

The Yoga of Marijuana

Oshadhis is an accelerated technique to Enlightenment fraught with many pitfalls along the way. While Yoga Masters warn against the sense of bliss and self-satisfaction that comes about in a stage preliminary to the highest state of meditation, i.e., total silence, stillness, without a sense of the personal self, that same complacency can overtake a student of Oshadhi, much more readily than on other paths. Because of the insight and lack of self-talk that occurs in *The Marijuana Consciousness*, there is the ego based judgment that one is much further along in the trip than is true, thereby utilizing the energy within the Plant for enjoyment, self-stroking and even arrogance rather than as an impetus to lose all personal identifications.

Even the kinship felt within the stigmatized community of Marijuana people can itself serve as diversion from the goal of self growth. To see beyond our ego driven motives requires that the student be extra vigilant to prideful thinking. A sense of smugness as an activist for the *cause* also is a distraction. The Path of Oshadhis is a solo mission, not suited to pleasure seekers. It is ignition of the desire for profound knowledge where worldly distractions and long-standing comfort levels are effortlessly shed. The trick in the mix is that one need not change either behavior or friends, but instead be *non-attached* to them. Oshadhi is primarily an inner practice; the externals need not change.

> *Be in the world But not of it* is the lesson for all serious seekers.
> (Krishnamurti)

The Yoga of Marijuana does not belong to the East or The West. It is the quintessence of a non-denominational and timeless course of seeking. At different periods of history, however, it has come forward in various pockets of the globe; nonetheless it always is present in the backdrop and in the fringes of civilizations. It is prehistoric yet it is modern. It comprises all classes of people. That the Path of Oshadhis is recognized in The Sutras is indicative of the thoroughness of the Indian tradition; while of course, it is appropriate acknowledgment of the consistent presence of the Sativa as it was incorporated into Indian culture, more so than in any other. Nevertheless in (Cannabis and The Soma Solution), Bennett substantiates that Cannabis *as Sacrament* was indeed prevalent across all the lands of old, although this reality is lost to time.

> *Oshadhi is not voluntarily chosen.*
> *It is a Predetermined Path for certain travelers.*
> *They meet continuously along the Road to Realization and*
> *Recognize by the Grace of the Sativa that they are following a*
> *Constant, Recurrent Path.* (Bello)

Marijuana - the Accelerator

Jeff Brown (Marijuana and The Bible) refers to Marijuana as an Accelerator, recognizing *The Marijuana Path* as an expedited, forceful, fortuitous and mysterious, long standing yet hidden Tradition of Yoga that sustains the **veteran seeker** along the journey of realization. By its inbuilt effects, *Marijuana* incites interest into the deepest dimension of existence; encourages tolerance; invites compassion; increases self-knowledge; and supports superior health. Regardless status, age or ethnicity, millions (possibly tens of millions) have been served by Marijuana as an awakening. They are the intrepid followers with a deep need/desire/capacity to attain to consciousness beyond what is usual but that is possible.

> *The Yoga of Marijuana*
> *Is The Fast Path to Enlightenment.*
> (Bello)

Manifestations of The Master Teacher: The Guru

Whereas the *Spirit in Marijuana* serves as an unseen but palpable guide that steers the student onward, the principle of Classical Yoga calls for an actual embodied human teacher, a *Master Yogi*, who escorts the aspirant to and through the *Mystery of Mystical Knowledge*. Once the seeker's interest has been ignited, after an appropriate period of study, either long or short, The Tradition of Yoga Science maintains that the *Guru* will automatically materialize. (*And for me, it was so.*) Such an inexplicable happenstance is nearly impossible for the contemporary orientation to accept. In fact, even the notion of an evolved person is an idea of fantasy for most Westerners.

> *Most modern practitioners know nothing*
> *about the moral disciplines*
> *... show little or no interest in meditation.*
> *The idea of a guru is alien.*
> *The concept of liberation is outlandish.* (Feuerstein)

> (In Sanskrit)
> The word Guru is a compound of two words, Gu and Ru.
> <u>Gu means darkness</u> and <u>Ru means light.</u>
> That which dispels the darkness of ignorance is called Guru.
> The energy and action of removing darkness are Guru.
> <u>Guru is not a person, it is a force driven by Grace.</u>
> (Swami Rama)

> It all depends on what you call a Guru... need not be human.
> Dattatreya had twenty-four Gurus,
> Including The Five Elements.
> Every object in this world was his Guru.
> (Sri Ramana Maharishi)

> Hidden in the Eminent <u>Sutras;</u>
> Referenced in the Prehistoric <u>Vedas,</u>
> The Teaching is Clear
> Once a certain plateau of development is attained,
> The Spirit of/in the Guru is all that is needed
> Whether embodied in a Person, a Dream, a Sound
> Or a Flower. (Bello)

Mind Field: Defined

To appreciate Yoga Science, it is crucial to understand that Yoga is a systematic method to peace and/or stillness in what is referred to as the *mind field* - likened to a dynamic energetic envelope surrounding the person. It can be in sync with the cosmic pulsation of silent potentiality or, as is the case with the normal human situation, vibrating in the movement/noise of constant thought. By its inherent nature, the mind is always flitting from one idea to another. The very precise language of Yoga Science refers to this continuous fluctuation as the *modifications of the mind field*. These modifications are seen as waves that distort perception. They are thoughts that stand between the essence of the person and reality. If stilled, we *See*, we *Awaken*, we *Realize*.

The modern hyped up lifestyle is very far from grasping such an idea. No attention is paid to the spiritual clarity inherent in silence, nor is there any comprehension of what that means and little, if any interest in finding out. The natural constant of thinking, such as of imagination, worry over life problems and planning pleasure is accepted. But wisdom comes from quiet, i.e., not thinking just observing, i.e., *stillness in the mind field*. We can compare the *mind field* to the corona of the sun which is just particulate matter of the sun itself. If each particle of the Source, thinks, it identifies itself as a separate entity, divided from the Sun. Its movement of thought necessarily obscures its own light. But with No thought, it is enlightened. People are no different. Thought, in all its diverse forms, obscures us from being Present to What Is.

Yoga is a step-wise science that teaches the first step to self development is awareness of the multiple thoughts that occur involuntarily, all the time. Such a state of mindfulness is a positive experience from which the leap to no thought is possible. Mindfulness can likewise be measured in the type of brain activity that takes place. Alpha waves of the brain are defined as relaxed alertness, subjectively felt as a *good mood*, as defined by the Institute of Medicine (IOM) in its description of the overall feature of *The Marijuana Consciousness*. Negative emotions, on the other hand, serve no function, other than to maintain the constant, cacophony in the mind field.

Every thought, is conveyed to the cells.
If there is confusion, depression and other negative emotions …they
are telegraphically transmitted through the nerves to every cell ….
Thoughts of worry and thoughts of fear …
Destroy the harmony…efficiency, vitality and vigour.
…Grief in the mind weakens the body.
…All negative thoughts are forerunners of disease.
(Swami Rama)

THE SUTRAS

"Yoga is Cessation of the Modifications of the Mind Field"

Thinking is a natural human activity borne of the existential fear of the unknown. Thinking is a protector from whatever is frightening. It keeps us from feeling scared or bad and keeps us from growing and knowing. In this understanding, *thought is always dualistic.* It is an unremitting ego-centered conflict between desire and actuality. Whether one has a good or bad experience, or image or situation or outlook is all considered *"thinking."* It is always concern with oneself. Preoccupation with *me/myself/I* is either in the forefront of thought or buried in the unconscious.

The normal human condition of the mind being thus occupied consciously and even at the subconscious level constitutes the energetic *noise of thinking*. In the Yogic perspective, thought, however subtle is nevertheless understood as the materia of manifest dense energy.

> *You must rise above pure thoughts*
> *And*
> *Attain the Supreme state of Thoughtlessness*
> (Swami Rama)

Although refinement of the personal vibration (above the state of self-concern) is not an aspiration of present day civilization, nevertheless, ascension to a higher state of *living and being*, is indisputably the ultimate fruition for humanity. The methods of Yoga Science show the way to *super-consciousness*, the state of stillness beyond thought where Love resides.

Yoga is the Anecdote to the Disease of Thought. (Bello)

Marijuana is a Foretaste of the Magic of Thoughtlessness.
(Bello)

The Lake

All practices of Yoga Science work to quiet the mind. Since it is very hard for the common person to comprehend what is meant by *No Thought,* Yoga teachers often use the example of a lake full of ripples. The bottom cannot be seen because the surface movement hides the view. The lake symbolizes the *mind field.* If the ripples of thoughts (*modifications*) dissipate, we can see into the depths. But it is not possible to imagine what we will see because imagining is a function of the mind. According to Patanjali, hindrances to quietude of mind are comprised of five types of thought: *correct understanding, false understanding, imagination, sleep* and *memory.* In other words, whether thought is positive or negative, in the realm of our awareness or not, thinking destroys silence/stillness.

To go beyond the mind is the invitation of Yoga to know the unknown. That is the *state of being* in which we are said to *realize the self (who we really are).* This is a fairly simple, logical explanation but for the most part it falls on deaf ears. The philosophy of *No thought* is hardly enticing to a striving world ensnared in the *cycle of pleasure and pain.* For those interested, Yoga Science is a tried and true method to Self-Realization. Defined as permanent happiness, it is an enduring state of being without thought, known as *undifferentiated consciousness.* In this state, there are no questions or doubts or hopes or fears. A person is self-contained. The energetic flitting is non-existent. There is no confusion. One is free from artificially imposed divisions of right and wrong and good and bad. Dualistic judgments of pleasure and pain dissolve with the *resolution of the opposites* as in *The Marijuana Consciousness.*

> *Pleasure and Pain are everlasting polarities*
> *With thought, there is desire,*
> *If there is desire, there is pain*

> *Desire filled is Pleasure. Ending of Pleasure is Pain*
> *Impressions of Desire rise one after another constantly.* (Bello)
> *Thought breeds fear*, according to the great sage, Krishnamurti.
> *Fear of tomorrow, of losing a job, of death, of falling ill, of pain:*
> *Fear implies a process of thought about the future or past.*
> *One is afraid of tomorrow or of what has been or what will be.*
> *What has brought fear? Isn't it thought? So thought breeds fear.*

Practically speaking, there are only relatively few people who make the connection between happiness and quiet mind; and fewer still who experience the relief of *No Thought*. Modern psychology actually works toward *positive thinking* rather than *not thinking*. But the cycle of thought is dualistic. Pleasure promises pain just as thinking good thoughts sets the future potential for negativity. In addition, the modern lifestyle of constant activity, entertainment and distraction is itself cause for the habit of continuous ups and downs of thinking.

The term *contemplating your navel* is an old derogation for being *spaced out* or *stoned* or for that matter, *meditating*, since in the materialistic orientation, all such introspective endeavours are shunned as unproductive deviant wastes of time. But for a growing minority, there is an irresistible impulse away from the sanctioned confusion toward a more meaningful reality. Modern jargon refers to such a state as *Being Present*, often reported in *The Marijuana Consciousness*, wherein thinking is paused and tranquillity emerges. One is in the state of being *a Centre of Observation of Now-ness and Newness*, without any thoughts of past or future. This is the *No Mind* that cannot be explained in words, but which Marijuana imparts freely and automatically to those who are receptive.

> *Not till your thoughts cease all their branching here and there,*
> *Not till you abandon all thoughts of seeking for something,*
> *Not till your mind is motionless as wood or stone,*
> *Will you be on the right road to the Gate."*
> (The Zen Teaching of Huang Po)

> *Be Awake. Be the Witness of Your Thoughts.*
> *You are What Observes, NOT What You Observe.*
> (Gautama Buddha)

The Science of Cannabis and Pausing The Mind

Science has proven an inherent beneficial psycho-bio-energetic link between Cannabis and humans. Specific to the altered consciousness with Marijuana is the increased time span between neuronal messaging in the brain which translates *as increased spaces between thoughts*. We now appreciate that the issue of how time seems to go slower, especially for the novice, when experiencing the effects of Marijuana early on, in fact has a biological construct. Thinking slower is a function of time being stretched out - so that the spaces in neuronal messaging are reflected from an empirical basis as less activity and therefore is interpreted from the habitual registration of the passage of time, as being slowed.

Half a century ago, the well-known psychological researcher, Charles Tart explained it as *slowing down of attentional shifts*. Since then, research with Marijuana has demonstrated that there is a measureable *toned down* messaging in the brain which explains the superior focusing and noticing of a specific topic as well as greater awareness, depth and appreciation of the enhanced cognition with Marijuana. Since less energy is spent flitting from one thought to another, there is naturally more energy that attends to the present.

Spaces of *no thought* are nano-second suspensions in the usual intervals of synaptic brain messaging and provide *time outs* from the daily fare of shallow interests. Simultaneously, a psychological receptivity to authentic values is encouraged, such as in creative flashes of intuition or acts of compassion borne of the heart. Pausing the usual mental chatter (*self-talk*) is freedom from the limited perspective of a separate self. Clarity emerges with decreased mental noise.

Practice of Yoga / Effects of Marijuana

The *Objective* of Yoga is very clear but the route to *silent mind* is intricate, long term and demanding. Sustained discipline is needed to learn the art of meditation. The student must become expert in disregarding the constant inner turmoil and ignoring myriad enticing external distraction. The aim of the arduous practices of Yoga compared with the natural outcome of regular application of Marijuana underscores their uncanny similarity. Without continuous thinking, the energy of the mind field is stilled, resulting in an unusually quiescent state referred to as *altered consciousness*. The subjectively registered psychological **pause in thinking** reflects the scientifically observed physiological *expanded cellular suspension* from Marijuana. From this space of silence comes the chance for an unbiased and global perspective which often allows for apprehending the mystical realm. For those who are receptive, lasting spiritual realization is the constant beguiling potential of *The Marijuana Consciousness*.

> *If I want to understand somebody,*
> *My mind must be quiet, Not chattering, Not prejudiced,*
> *Not having innumerable opinions or experiences*
> *For they prevent the observation and the understanding.*
> *... It is only when the mind is very quiet that there is... clarity;*
> *The purpose of meditation is to bring about such a state.* (Krishnamurti)

Meditation and Pausing Thought

The effects of Marijuana on thinking have their counterpart in studies with meditating Masters demonstrating simultaneous suspension of brainwaves with lengthened intervals between neuronal activities. In fact, research into meditation shows that the usually busy brain wave patterns are slowed as the sought after calmness infiltrates the body. Subjectively, such a result is registered as ascension to awe and peace and a sense of well-being. As a permanent feature of the person, it is called Enlightenment; limited to a time frame, we call it *Getting High*.

*The Effortlessness by which Marijuana Enhances The Breath
Is the Secret to its Kinship with Yoga Science
Breathing with inhibition and tension causes loss of awareness.
Breathing regularly with fullness and ease raises consciousness.*
(Bello)

The Connection between Body and Mind through *The Breath*
Is Basic to Eastern Metaphysics and Medicine.

*There is Intimate Connection
Between Thinking and Respiration.
When the Mind is Concentrated, Breathing Becomes Slow.
If one Thinks Fast the Respiration also Becomes Fast.*
(Swami Rama)

<u>The Breath</u> is an all-inclusive term in Yoga Science with both spiritual and health overtones. The Hindu term for breath is *Prana*. It can be translated in any number of ways, such as, air, breathing, wind, vitality, even the tendency toward a type of personality. In the context at hand, it is best understood as the *vital essence* in the environment or that which imparts life. The manner in which we breathe determines the amount, degree and strength of the vivifying force that we can utilize.

*The reciprocal character of Mind and Prana
…Means that a certain type of mind, or mental activity,
Is invariably accompanied by a Prana
Of corresponding character and rhythm
…Reflected in the phenomenon of Breathing.*

*… Anger produces…an inflamed thought-feeling,
But also a harsh and accentuated roughness of breathing.*

*On the other hand,
When there is calm concentration,
ght and the breathing exhibit a like calmness.
ncentration is deep…the breath is held.* (C. C. Chang)

*...In a mood of anger, pride, envy, shame, arrogance, love, lust, (etc.)
This particular Prana or air can be felt immediately within oneself.*

Every mood, thought, and feeling whether simple, subtle, or complex
Is accompanied by a corresponding or reciprocal Prana.
(C. C. Chang)

To recharge the body, to increase one's lifespan, to boost the healing capacity of the organism from all illness, and most notably, to raise consciousness, Yoga teaches techniques (*Pranayama*) to expand, enhance and fine tune the efficacy of breathing. Unfortunately, it has yet to be studied in the West except in Psychiatry where research with the pathologies has discovered that dysfunction in breathing wields significant influence on mental stability. In the Psychiatric texts, the link between repressed respiration and neurotic and/or psychotic behavior has been taught for decades. Nevertheless, treatment still revolves around dealing with problematic feelings and actions instead of instruction to restore the breath to health.

But the *Eastern (wholistic) Medical Model* that has seeped into the modern world as Holistic Health holds as its first tenet to restore the body/mind to harmony, logically accomplished by ferreting out the cause of imbalance (dis-ease) rather than treating symptoms. *The Pattern of The Breath* is the premier measure of health, i.e., *Balance*. All limiting factors to the way a person inhales and exhales **regularly**, over a lifetime have consequences in kind to health. When the body is sick, it is mirrored in the breathing habit, in the same way that mental illness is echoed in *The Pattern of The Breath*, however subtly.

*Every depressing and disturbing thought
That enters your brain,
Has a depressing effect on every cell of your body,
And tends to produce disease*
(Swami Rama)

49

Re-establishing *The Breath* to be effortlessly full, even and silent (as at birth) is the goal of Yoga Science, since it directly parallels, is cause *for* and is caused *by* Higher Consciousness. Therefore, one of the most important practices in Yoga Science is learning ways to free the Pattern of The Breath.

> To the extent that we enhance <u>*The Pattern of The Breath*</u>,
> We improve the health of body and mind and free the spirit.

<u>Marijuana Enhances the Pattern of the Breath Immediately</u>.

The superior *Pattern of the Breath* (as occurs with Marijuana) has spiritual benefits known since antiquity that are lost to our world. Science does not appreciate the correlation between body, mind and spirit. In fact, it prides itself on being secular without recognizing the existence of a non-corporeal essence. On the other hand, the Science of Yoga knows that the <u>Liberated Breath **is** Enlightenment</u> and is also *Its* result. *Pranayama* is ancient, yet at the same time, it is *state-of-the-art*, systematic training specifically geared to free *The Breath* from its habitual inhibition.

While breathing is usually automatic, we can supersede the mechanical process and pay attention to the way we breathe so that it is relaxed, even and full, although, unfortunately we cannot do it for very long. Thoughts intrude mechanically into our intended attentiveness; so that the characterological and limiting tendency returns. Only in the *Super-Consciousness* state, known as *Enlightenment, Beatific Vision, Self-Realization, The Void, Nirvana, Samadhi* or, as Krishnamurti describes it: a *complete revolution of the mind, is The Pattern of The Breath* unperturbed because there are no thoughts. Mind is silent.

> *Do naught with the body but relax,*
> *Shut firm the mouth and silent remain,*
> *Empty your mind and think of naught* (Swami Sivananda)

The Pattern of the Breath is not only a measure of our overall health (physical and mental), but is a subtle, accurate indicator of personality. Particulars of restricting the breath are unique and yet serve to classify us all. Generally, there is the *chest breather* who is nervous; the *subdued breather* who is depressed; and the *uneven breather* who is sick. Some people breathe paradoxically, i.e., the diaphragm moves up (when it should move down) and the stomach expands (instead of contracting) during exhalation. This is the signature of schizophrenia.

Regardless of the shortcoming of the *pattern*, in a civilized society of constant taming and training, just about every adult is a dysfunctional breather. The relaxed, full, silent regular *breath* is unfortunately, usually only seen in early life, whereas no one who has internalized the prejudice of family, tribe or society is free - given that the *conditioning of separateness* manifests as discord throughout the whole organism, as body nervousness, mental discontent, and, of course, restricted breathing. The whole array of disruptions is unfortunately conveyed down through the generations, osmotically, i.e., to our children, so that the same specifics of imbalance or lack of ease (dis-ease) very often are prevalent in families.

> *Parents are trapped by the concept of what a perfect child would be .... People begin to live for an ideal (and) lose the natural, slow Rhythm of Life (and Breath). It's a cultural thing.*
> (Marion Woodman)

Enculturation Means that the Culture is In Us!

> *In freedom, there is no judgment as to how things should be.*
> *There is no desire to change the way things are.*
> *All conditioning is shed. Self-identification is absent.*
> *Fear is non-existent. Breath is full*
> *Mind is silent.*
> (Bello)

Any of these conditions designates the ability to see clearly. Yoga teaches that the most efficient path to freedom is by way of *The Breath* rather than working on the vagaries of the mind or the unbridled world of emotions.

Breath is the Bridge which Connects Life to Consciousness,
...Unites your Body to your Thoughts.
Whenever your Mind Becomes Scattered, Use your Breath
To Take Hold of your Mind Again. (Thich Nhat Hanh)

The undisciplined mind is worried, uptight, on guard and fearful which corresponds directly to the degree of inhibition of *The Breath*. It is an affectation that affects us all. It is an unrecognized axiom that whatever disturbance exists at the psychological level will be accompanied by restriction in the *Pattern of the Breath*. The reverse is equally true. The breathing dysfunction reflects the degree of mental insecurity. For the holistic practitioner trained in *reading the breath*, the foibles of the personality are all too clear. Juxtaposed to this reality is the understanding that release of restraint in the breathing process results in dissolution of the uncertainty in the mind.

Marijuana Enhances the Pattern of The Breath Immediately.

No doubt there are many ways to ascend to a higher plateau of living and being. In Yoga, the first *must* is an unwavering desire to evolve beyond the habitually divided Mind; one of the most effective ways is by way of Pranayama, i.e., the practice of learning to enhance **The Pattern of The Breath**. Comforts of contemporary life, unending entertainment, physical security and/or wealth cannot impart the inner sense of well-being of breathing naturally when the mind is quiet. At this time in our history, it seems as though society is at the furthest pole imaginable from this kind of inner peace.

Nevertheless, there is an Aroma of Anticipation in the Air.

The People found the Way:

Not the doctors, theologians or psychologists recognize that health of the body, mind and spirit is correlated directly to diminished thought which in turn translates as unrestricted breathing, expressed in turn in a compassionate attitude. But in the past half century, a great proportion of the lay population has come to this knowledge by way of their own experience with Marijuana. The felt sense of well-being; relief from chronic medical problems; along with personal and frequent encounters of expanded awareness have exposed the healing reality of silence. *The Yoga of Marijuana* has gathered its community of like-minded travelers who are carrying out the contemporary *reweaving* to the spaces between thoughts. Regardless the overall darkness, the Holy Books of Old all promise such an intersection for possible growth.

The Flower of Consciousness Leads the Way. (Bello)

The Legend of the Origin of Marijuana

The heightened awareness and increased vitality imparted by Marijuana is why it has been such an enduring ally for humans. While the supreme compatibility of Marijuana molecules with the body is now proven scientifically, this knowledge is not new. *The Churning of The Cosmic Ocean* (Milky Way) is the Indian legend that recounts the primal creation when gods and demons worked together to release the elixir of immortality (*Amrita*) from the planetary soup.

O ye gods, churn the Ocean, ye will discover amrita. (The Vedas)

As the story goes, numerous elements were forcefully expelled by the constant churning over eons of time, such as gods, goddesses, animals, planetary bodies, as well as an overwhelming poison (very closely paralleling the current theory of the origin of the universe).

At length the prize so madly sought,
The Amrit, to their sight was brought. (The Vedas)

Once the Amrita had been released, a grand battle to capture the treasure arose between the gods and demons with the gods being the victors. For some mysterious reason there was need to purify the Elixir so The Great Lord created Cannabis from his own body. A similar version of the origin of Bhang is that it sprang as the plant we know, sown from a body part (perhaps a rib) of Mahadeva (Great God) known from that time forward as *Lord of Bhang*. Both versions acknowledge the supernatural benefits of Marijuana as well as the intention of its creation so as to *give great joy to the people*.

But what is most revealing for us is that a myth that survived thousands of years and speaks to a time yet further back than is conceivable refers to Cannabis as *Body Born* recognizing its utter compatibility with humankind.

This fantastic tale speaks to a state of *freedom from fear* and with the possibility of merging with the purest vibration. Such an enlightened attitude is lost to modern sophistication, but it harkens back to the Western culture's fable of Adam and Eve. Regardless the broad range of differences between Eastern and Western worlds, legends of both refer to an idealized past when thinking was suspended, worry was non-existent and the *super conscious* state was honored. Although the major society is disinterested in any such spiritual potential, there is a steady movement toward the reality that cannot be stilled.

Marijuana Enhances The Breath;
Stills the Energetic Dissonance of the Mind Field;
Relaxes the Musculature
Allowing for Conscious Participation in Mundane Existence
And Into the Innate Morality of an Awakened Conscience.
(Bello)

Health, Spiritual Ripening, Interest and Intentionality

Health of body and mind is a prerequisite to spiritual practice. Consciousness arises from positive energy. Only from the launch pad of both physical and mental balance, evidenced in regularity in the breathing pattern is there even the slightest chance for individual evolution. In this paradigm, *Health* implies mental equanimity accompanied by toned down biological reactivity, no doubt an attainable goal via sincere and constant Yoga practice, although, as we have seen in this *day and age*, a difficult course to master. In contrast, regular entrance into *The Marijuana Consciousness* serves as a natural, safe passage to holistic health. That is, if the recipient has the capacity to integrate the refined energy of the plant.

Interest into Life Mysteries obviously is a precondition for study toward refining one's vibration. Not everyone is so inclined. There are many theories regarding the undeniable tendency for esoteric curiosity that singles people out from the crowd. *Karmic Ripening*, *Old Soul* and *Magnetic Center* are ascribed to those in search of the nonmaterial undercurrent. According to the traditional teaching, every sentient being will eventually reach such a plateau, whether in the present or in some future embodiment* so that being a candidate for *self-knowledge* is under the umbrella of *real time* readiness.

*Note: The most famous philosophy for deliverance of every soul is the Buddhist Teaching of the Enlightened *Bodhisattva*. *The Bodhisattva Vow* is taken by a veteran seeker of superior development who promises to put aside his/her own release from the world until all lesser souls have found their way. In a more mundane understanding, the vow can be interpreted as simply not putting oneself first and instead working for the good of all, always with the mysterious understanding that there is really Only the One manifest as Many:

May I attain Buddhahood for the Benefit of all Sentient Beings.

That *The Breath be unencumbered and the Mind still/silent is* the ideal. Realistically, *growth to the spirit* is usually a sequential climb with markers or energetic weigh stations (*chakras*) along the road that depict the vibrational progression. To begin the process, however, an abiding **Intention is essential**.

Intention: *One-pointedness* is a common Yogic description of meditation. It describes the uninterrupted flow of mental energy toward an object whatever that may be. During the initial process, the student learns to bring the naturally wandering mind back to the chosen object of focus until at some point during the arduous practice, the mind learns the trick of letting itself go and enters the realm of *No Thought*. Meditation is the end product of introspection, contemplation and concentration, all of which are stages of uncoupling from identification with the separate self to become a center of pure observation that appreciates the Unity of everything.

Full, deep and true meditation does not come easy. It is a rare state of being that identifies the individual who transcended *the mind*. It is the reward at the end of the journey which, according to the Yogic Tradition, will take many embodiments from the starting gate. When the *interest* is sufficiently piqued; when the *personality* is suitably groomed; the *will* sufficiently strong and the *body* is without distracting discomfort, then the time will have arrived when the student may qualify for consideration for the initial entry into the elite journey to self-realization. All that is needed at this level of readiness is the full intent of the individual seeker; where *full* has all the features of true meditation.

> *...The serious pursuit of the Yogic Ideal*
> *Is a Difficult Task*
> *(It) Cannot be undertaken as a mere Hobby,*
> *(As) an Escape from the Stress and Strain of ordinary Life.*
> (Taimini)

It (Meditation) *can be Undertaken only on Understanding Fully*
The Nature of Human Life
The Misery and Suffering Inherent In It
And the Further Realization
That the Only Way to End Suffering Permanently
Is to find the Truth Enshrined Within Ourselves.
(Taimini)

The intention to delve into non-material aspects of existence toward the principle that upholds all of life can come about in a number of ways, such as, through an immediate life-altering shock to long-held conditioned perceptions about the world, or as an almost unnoticed gradual progression over the course of the life-term. For some, it is part and parcel of the make-up from earliest memory. For others, it may be a re-gathering of childhood curiosity that was lost along the worldly way.

Regardless of cause, once the lock to the hidden dimension is tripped, the **intention** to understand becomes a paramount power in which little else is held in the highest regard. Once acknowledged and embraced, there is what can be called a *stretching* toward wisdom. The personality is (in a state of) yearning to be free which takes the form of a choiceless search for the unfoldment of consciousness.

Now, the Objective of Yoga
Is the Highest Prize of Human Achievement.
... Its pursuit must necessarily be very exacting
In its demand on the time and energy of the seeker.

That is why in olden days
People who wanted to Practice Yoga
Retired into forests
So that they could
Devote Themselves Completely to this task.
(Taimini)

57

Although contemporary life is unsuited to solitary living, the precept of evolution to the next plane of development always relies on an inherent magnetic compass to Reality. Nothing in the knowledge of all time can impart such an attunement. But there are triggers that are often credited with firing its passion. **The Marijuana Experience is one such spark.**

> *We Drank Bhang and the Mystery ... Grew Plain.*
> *The Soul in whom the Spirit of Bhang finds a Home*
> *Glides into the Ocean of Being*
> *Freed from the weary round of matter-blinded self.* (The Vedas)

> *Yoga is an Experiential Science of Self-Discipline.*
> *It steers the seeker from self-absorbed thinking.*
> *Be Still and Know Thy God is the Biblical equivalent.*
> *It is also the Experience of The Marijuana Consciousness.*
> (Bello)

Features of Yoga and History of Marijuana

Motivation for Yoga is as old as the human race, yet as relevant today as at its outset. It is a timeless path that speaks to the soul-goal of all who are compelled to look beyond the illusion. *The Message of Yoga* is constant, comforting reassurance that *freedom from fear* is the ultimate inherent inheritance for us all. *The Promise of Yoga* is hierarchical ascension to ever deeper self-discovery accomplished by intricate life-long, time-worn mind/body training whereby mind is no longer cluttered. *Instructions for Yoga* are intensely detailed, that, if followed in good faith have guaranteed, although not immediate results. The *Goal of Yoga* is profound and addresses a state of being usually not sought or expected but universally revered; while *The Origin of Yoga* is lost to time but its secrets are embedded as permanent archetypes in the psyche of the human species. *The Purpose of Yoga* is removal of suffering to allow for the bliss of reality thereby infusing life with joy and fearlessness.

> *Yoga teaches*
> *That to be born human is a blessing.*
> *Yoga means union...connects body with mind, breath and soul.*
> (Rajmani)

The Philosophy of Yoga has no recorded beginning which just adds to the mystery. The Teaching is that the knowledge of how to raise one's vibration from self-centeredness to full awareness was conveyed from teacher to student through civilizations so long ago that there are no traces. Only the wisdom remains. It is still accessed and displayed by adept Yogis who continue to astound contemporary technology.

The Marijuana Consciousness Predates The Science of Yoga
Modern scientific **research** concerning the interface between Marijuana molecules (*cannabinoids*) and the human body; as well as **botanical knowledge; historical evidence; personal experience; objective observation,** including **integration of all relevant research**, indicates that purposeful invoking of *The Marijuana Consciousness* **preceded the formal practice of Yoga by (hundreds of) thousands of years (or more)**.

Indeed, if we accept the wealth of scientific evidence proving the beneficial effects of Marijuana, for both body and mind; and are knowledgeable concerning the latest research with the plant cannabinoids and their interaction with the physiology of our organisms; and if we are without prejudice regarding the co-evolution of this ancient plant with the human species; and also if we understand the extraordinarily exceptional intended ultimate aim of Yoga, there is little rationale against accepting that Cannabis Sativa served as the originating impetus for Yogic Science and its practice. This historical interface is the subject matter of the Second Part of this presentation: <u>The Tantra of Marijuana.</u>

From the records of the ancient Indian world, dated some 10,000 years ago, we have evidence that Bhang was revered unconditionally. Scripture from that era, however refers to prior knowledge of the treasures of Bhang yet further back in time than is imaginable which suggests a connection with our specie far stronger and longer ago than can be verified. We can only surmise that the relationship between Marijuana and the peoples from even before the dawn of recorded history emerged quite naturally from an uncensored intuition prior to cultural judgment that came into play with the development of politically structured communities.

The Vedas are the oldest scripture, far older than Patanjali's Sutras (dated 3000 years ago). Amazingly the teachings of the prehistoric Vedas had precise knowledge of planetary positions that have been confirmed to a time well before what the Western world considers the period of caveman. Officially, The Vedas are credited with being possibly 10,000 years old. Its mysterious knowledge before that time is simply ignored.

The Lost and Found City of Harappan

The most advanced civilization uncovered to date was the Harappan society already a thriving civilization at least 3000 years ago, which we must acknowledge that its hundreds of sophisticated surrounding cities, probably took thousands of years to construct and develop long before becoming what archeologists finally unearthed. The **megapolis** of Harappan was located between India and Pakistan, in total comprising 1,052 cities and villages. Its sister city, Mohenjo-Daro shared the identical type construction, organized urban planning, without evidence of either palaces or military operations indicating a peaceful, egalitarian society that traded with the surrounding societies. Gold, copper, pottery, incense burners have been uncovered throughout these ancient yet amazingly developed civilizations.

The Yugas of Eastern Metaphysics

Western cosmology is measured in linear time. But in the East, the nature of the universe is considered as infinitely recurring cycles of creation and dissolution. When we speak of Yoga Science as a codified teaching, just thousands of years old, that orientation is taken from the limits of the reigning era. To fathom Indian time, look to the *Yuga* that describes a particular period of set duration. Yugas resemble seasons as there are four phases. The current Yuga is *Kali* that can be likened to the *Winter of the Discontent of Humanity* when wisdom, life span, intellect and even stature are at only **25%** capacity. When this present impoverishment of spirit ends, thankfully virtue and peace will return. *Satya Yuga* represents the renewal period of wisdom wherein virtue and compassion are at their height of a full 100%. It follows Kali and mercifully lasts four times as long as our present *epoch*. *Treta Yuga* follows Satya where human attributes are diminished by only 25%; *Dvapara Yuga* is next when there is a 50% decline.

The 5100th year of Kali Yuga corresponds to 2,000 A.D. This age will continue for more than 400,000 years.

These cycles continue till the end of this universe, billions of years hence when all manifestation is swept away, possibly into a Black Hole of oblivion until the next rebirth.

A Popular Hindu Tale to Boggle the Imagination

The vast difference between the Indian way of thinking and the Western point of view as regards time is easily seen in this popular Hindu myth:

> An Immortal Eagle who Brushes the Tops
> Of the Himalayan Mountains with a Feather
> Only every 1,000 Years would erode the mountains
> In the same amount of time
> That the present manifestation has so far existed.

The Bridge Before History (named Adam's Bridge)

The modern mind does not include any possibility of such vastness of time, so we assume such stories are just symbolic for effect. But an astonishing scientific discovery made just a little over a decade ago suggests otherwise. In 2002 photos from a NASA shuttle from outer space located a *man-made bridge* between India and Sri Lanka. The scientific estimate is that it had been constructed roughly **1,700,000 years ago.** Western Science, however, dates the entry of humans on the planet from only 200,000 years?

If we look to Indian Scripture, such as, the ancient <u>Ramayana</u> or the sacred <u>Srimad-Bhagavatam</u>, we find an actual account of the building of this very bridge. According to the tale, it took place during The *Treta* Yuga (nearly two million years ago) when people had godlike powers or when there were gods among the people. What is especially eerie is that the laborers who built the bridge were reportedly monkey-like hominids (in keeping with modern accounting) who were guided by superior beings. What is weirder yet, is that both these ancient texts are only 5000 years old. We are left with the question: *How* could that society (of 5000 years ago) have knowledge of a bridge with its correct location and details of construction 1,699,500 years in its past?

Only extra-sensory abilities or superior consciousness are possibilities. In other words, statistics that are impossible to know without technology were indeed known! The more we investigate, the more precise information is found.

With deep respect, I bow to the sun,
Who travels 2,202 yojanas in half a nimesha.
(Hymn from Rig Veda by Sayana)

(That value calculates at 185,794 mps or virtually the 186,000 miles per second of modern calculation.)

Sutra 3:26-28 explains that perception from *concentration, meditation* and *unbroken mental absorption* on the sun, moon and pole star imparts knowledge of the planets and stars.

Sutra 3:33 states: *Through keenly developed intuition, everything can be known.*

In India, these are universally accepted truths from the past that are also embodied in living examples. This cannot be fully appreciated without having encountered an evolved person, known as a *Living Master.* To have been in the company of a full-fledged enlightened Yogi is an unforgettable blessing that leaves no doubt whatsoever of the possible heights of human evolution. Such an encounter is rare in the West, but in the East, it is a common experience for a great majority of citizens. Of course, there are charlatans (and many of them) and many of them have migrated toward material gain. But there are definitely those Yogis with a palpable aura of peace and wisdom who are unmistakably *for real.*

In addition to the greater likelihood that a seeker from India has met (or at least been in the presence of) a Master Teacher, there is also the constant retelling of the ancient scriptures in theaters and readings popular from childhood which lends familiarity with the ideals of *self-realization and endless time,* about which, for the most part, our society has no training.

Accepting the high tech proof of the prehistoric bridge was a matter of course for the sophisticated and broad-minded Indian teaching which combines ultra-modern precepts with the ancient scripture so effortlessly. That is because revelation garnered from deep meditation is unconditionally respected in India. Invisible mysteries are understood as simply representing and upholding that which is visible. Material evidence serves only as validation of limitless possibilities.

The West, in contrast relies solely on the material measure. Its heritage has no abiding historical or spiritual tradition that delves beneath the surface. Objective science reigns. Ironically, when it came to concrete evidence of the prehistoric bridge, an irresolvable conflict existed. The discovery was diametrically opposed to ingrained science. While Indian news reported the reality of the bridge with little fanfare, it was ignored in the West. The materialistic ethic has a built in abhorrence to the unexplained. Within every society however, there are those who are drawn beyond usual boundaries.

The Perpetual Search
The quest to uncover the secrets of existence is a continuous ebb and flow along the timeline of our race that resonates with the energetic vibration of the particular era. In the footprints of our ancestors, there is legend of before the path to higher consciousness was lost. Indeed, all ancient philosophies teach the possible returning to what at one idyllic time was a state of enlightenment, peace and happiness. Through endless eons, the legacy of the *key to the mystery* is a perpetual stream that meanders hidden within the major culture uncovering buried mysterious remnants and tucking them away for a later time when the treasure may be again embraced.

> The current is normally beneath the surface,
> Its very existence unsuspected
> Save by those who…immersed themselves in it.
> But the continuation is proved
> …From time to time it breaks forth from its confines
> Surges into full view, surprising and alarming
> The general population - the orthodox of every faith. (King)

As humans stray ever further from their birthright, there is an inevitable pull back to that lost reality. A choiceless wave of inspired seekers resists the ingrained ignorance and responds to the uptick in *the tempo of the times* to fulfill *The Tradition*.

Moments in History That Matter

Such a moment is now. The possibility of being more than embroiled in antagonism and selfishness is overpowering to those of us who have glimpsed the truth by *Marijuana*. Not only are we naturally drawn to the deeply-felt *release and relief via the enrichment of the experience* but there is a compelling shared understanding that from liberation of the mind with all its artificial conditioning, the next stage for humankind, i.e., *Evolution to the Spirit is ensured.* No longer inhibited by way of the gross vibration of fear, *The Marijuana Consciousness* is an effortless ascension to a *privileged plateau of knowing.*

> *The Marijuana Consciousness is a State of Familiar Magic.*
> *It is also a welcomed summoning back to a long forgotten*
> *Archetypal encounter that registers as Eternal and is*
> *Intuitively sensed as Mysteriously Recurrent.*
> (Bello)

> ***The Yoga of Marijuana*** *is an Unbroken Tradition.*
> *As a Practice, It is Older than Antiquity.*
> *Usually Hidden from the Exoteric Circle of Mundane Life,*
> *Nevertheless, It Has Always Been Available,*
> *For Those Who Are Perpetually Drawn To It.*
> (Bello)

Yoga of Marijuana: Collective Turning Toward the Essential

Until now, *The Yoga of Marijuana* has been an *Unnamed Global Movement* of youth and old alike who know that Marijuana is of joyful assistance on their counter-culture journey. Since esoteric curiosity is inborn and undeniable, the yearning for authenticity is not the result of altered consciousness. It is an inherent impression within the individual. While the invisible world is dismissed by the existing social structure and any experience with the non-material dimension is discouraged, even prohibited, it matters not to the determined searcher.

Eternal Mysteries Plead for Solutions.
As an Intuitive Realization, Marijuana Translates the Undercurrent
of Dissatisfaction that Plagues the Mind.
(Bello)

The Pause is the Doorway to Intelligence

Yoga explains the energetic changes that take place through sustained practice that impart health benefits to the organism, including the development of the personality. Ironically, fortuitously, predictably and magically, those very same benefits are conveyed by T*he Marijuana Consciousness*. What happens in the mind, *the breath* and the cells of the body with Marijuana is perfectly in step with the state of *self-realization* as outlined in Yoga. For millions of people, now and down through the folds of time, Marijuana has responded to the sense that something essential is missing.

By its inherent feature of Expanding the Pattern of the Breath,
Marijuana increases oxygenation, relaxes the body,
Meanwhile calming the mind and comforting the yearning.
The Big Secret to Consciousness:
Is Spelled Out in Yoga,
Experienced with Marijuana
Completely Misunderstood by the Greater Culture.
(Bello)

Cannabis Sativa: Science and The Plant

Plants which as receptacles of light
Were born three ages before the Gods.
(The Vedas)

Botanically, Cannabis Sativa is classified with angiosperms (*seed-bearing plants*) that without any evolutionary clues quite inexplicably appeared some 200 or so million years ago, which is very long before the ancestors of Homo sapiens whose emergence on the planet can only be detected less than a million years ago. In fact, what is considered as scientific proof of the appearance of our distinct specie is only 30,000 years old. Lost to antiquity are the meandering traces that we share from any original life forms generated from the initial soup of life. Nevertheless, science has pieced together the genealogical tree that bears resemblance to our ancestral vertebrates, which diverged from the foremost group of sea animals some 800 million years ago.

Quite mysteriously, the THC receptor was conserved in all animals through eons of evolution. Admittedly, it is equally mystifying that this universal receptor was only discovered in the latter part of the 20th Century; and when finally uncovered by contemporary researches, initially its only function seemed to link with the phytochemicals of Cannabis Sativa. (Now, of course, we know that there is a *Cannabinoid System*, and that it is impacted by the Plant's (exogenous) cannabinoids as well as those cannabinoids produced within the body itself, and further that this entire network is the major modulating network of the organism. That this multi-tasking System was preserved through different specie for over 600 million years should serve to humble our overgrown sense of uniqueness, simultaneously evoking awe in the fact that Cannabis shares an uncanny and primordial compatibility with our biology.

67

The Interface of Cannabis Sativa With The Human Organism:

Marijuana conveys a smattering of the most powerful energy in the galaxy to those who partake of its magic. The Cannabis Sativa Plant is unique in that it can take in ultraviolet rays and incorporate them into its own *one-of-a-kind* plant compounds. No other vegetation does this. In fact, ultra violet emissions are too powerful to be utilized directly by most vegetation; and usually damage or completely destroy plant life as well as many earth creatures. Whether through Divine intervention, co-evolution or convenient accident, the super-regulatory system of most animals is strangely well-matched with the exceptional, solar infused cannabinoids from Marijuana.

The Cannabis System

The Cannabinoid System is a network of messenger cells and receptors in all the organs, systems and tissues of vertebrates (some non-vertebrates) of the planet. It is far older than our specie, having been conveyed to our predecessors before they could even be considered human, yet is runs just about every biological function needed for life. How modern science with its technological precision missed its existence for so long remains a mystery. Most likely: The Cannabinoid System was overlooked because it is exceedingly delicate in its modus operandi, similarly understated in its effects and intricately indirect at the cellular level.

What is relevant to the discussion at hand is that the active molecules of Cannabis Sativa key into the Endocannabinoid System of our bodies in a completely compatible way. The Cannabinoid System was named because of its affinity and attraction for the compounds in Cannabis. Naturally, once science discovered its existence, it was clear that there must be a hormone produced by/in the body itself, specifically for interaction with its own network.

More studies found the *Endogenous* (*body built*) Cannabinoids. Because its mental effects were akin to the pleasurable *High* of THC, it was called, Ananda(mide) after the Sanskrit word for Bliss (*Ananda*). Anandamide was discovered first but science has now isolated a few other cannabinoids produced by the body. What is far more interesting is that many, many more phyto-chemicals from the Plant (known as the Exogenous *Cannabinoids*) have been isolated and shown to key into the receptors of the *Endo*-Cannabinoid System and they impact it with great synergistic energy. These compounds, which are now approaching 100, are being studied diligently by the pharmaceutical giants because so far every Plant Cannabinoid (exclusive to Cannabis), has demonstrated an unbelievably extensive list of healthful, restorative benefits, bordering on magic. It is no surprise that the Legal Drug Industry intends to exploit these natural healing compounds for its own profit, while resisting all efforts to allow legal freedom of the Plant.

Why is the Cannabis Sativa Plant so overwhelmingly helpful to the human organism?

We see a great compatibility with this ancient medicinal herb and our whole beings. We know our lives are more harried and striving and difficult than we would design them to be. Rich or poor, old, young, male or female, we all want more than we have or something different, or for more time or less. There is no end to our inner dissatisfaction. Meanwhile, our body/mind is being stressed from without as well. The food is unhealthy, as is the air, the water, the rushing lifestyle, etc. Our biology and psychology are obviously under assault, most of the time. The long and short of it is: our whole being, individually (and as a race), is out of balance which causes the unhealthy way in which we (all) breathe. We are stressed, simply the definition of imbalance in Holistic Health and the reason that the Endo-Cannabinoid System needs help to carry out its all important functions of *moderating, modulating and regulating* the organism to its fullest. (IOM, 1999)

Stress Dysregulates The Cannabinoid System,
From which a cascade of sickness results.

Marijuana Compounds restore The Cannabinoid System
To its Natural Balance with added Vitality and Strength.

It is that simple! It is the reason that Marijuana is an effective remedy for innumerable medical problems. It is also why on the whole, Marijuana imparts, a *sense of well-being* so defined by the government's own Institute of Medicine (IOM) study in 1999. The flowers, the leaves, even the roots of Marijuana share perfect cellular harmony with humans suggesting a dynamic biological interception not yet understood between the Animal and Vegetable Kingdoms. This shared molecular compatibility is indicated visibly in the feelings and attitudes of *well-being, tolerance* and *broad mindedness* along with an *energized serenity.* However, although we know that Marijuana is good for us, we cannot really answer the question *why* unless we enter the realm of the mystics.

General Benefits of Marijuana
Marijuana relaxes chronically armored muscles and loosens the habitual restriction in the *pattern of the breath* which is definitely a turning toward health. Yet witnessing the façade behind what we present to the world and even to ourselves (as occurs with the loss of our normal conditioned inhibitions) is an intimidating and humbling experience. Jeff Brown in Marijuana and The Bible, references the ancient plant as *The Humiliator*, an apt term for exposing the self-delusions we all harbor and shrink from when seen. No doubt, the illegality of Marijuana and the fear thereof contribute to the oft reported fright that comes over many novices with Marijuana. However, being stripped of pretenses and defenses, a natural consequence of fuller awareness, is what is mainly responsible for the *paranoia* that is triggered when the truth is outed.

The extent and depth of our hidden demons determines the degree of the paranoid reaction that may erupt. Nevertheless, to face our bare selves is a necessary, if sometimes painful but ultimately rewarding development. Luckily, regular jaunts into reality implemented via Marijuana allow for growth in self-knowledge without the initial shock that can cause the short lived distress.

At long last, the harmony between Cannabis *cannabinoids* with the body is being studied. However, what this means in terms of advancing the base nature of humans beyond self-centered emotions and antagonistic behavior has yet to be imagined.

Today we have more stuff and less wisdom. By the measure of human evolution, our specie has lost its essential impetus. Our reflective, curious nature is constantly purposefully distracted by the consequence of always being occupied, and never idle. The world looms as an arena of constant competition. As if on cue, the comfort and introspection derived from Cannabis has insinuated itself into the cacophony.

> *It Heightens the senses, yet paradoxically Quiets all systems.*
> *It Restores functionality to deranged tissue.*
> *It Lessens Pain.*
> *It Regulates The Breath which Re-vitalizes the organism.*
> (Bello)

Marijuana is loved for uplifting our moods, clarifying our thoughts and enhancing our consciousness. It is feared by those worried about losing power and those afraid to face reality. Despite worldwide persecution of *Marijuana People*, we are resolutely reunited with our abiding earth partner. This *Plant of Many Uses*, utilized by our *forefathers* (and Mothers) and our ancestors for every imaginable purpose, having been stamped out and desecrated time and time again, is very much with us as we go forward in the 21st Century.

Dualism of Body and Mind

The Marijuana Consciousness is a higher perspective than is our usual self-centeredness. Normally, we think in the *either/or* mode of personal survival and not the *both/and* inclusiveness of unity. The infant early on perceives the *Either* You *Or* Me polarity. Schism colors everything. We judge between *this and that* in sync with the circuitry of the bifurcated brain.

> *Modern Medical Science enumerates some nearly 4,000 diseases of the body and mind. Yoga views this vast proliferation of diseases as a natural outcome of the stress and strain of desire, fostered by modern propaganda...condoned on all sides even by religion science and philosophy...(with)the possibility of endless disorders. Disease is created...when duality arises in the human mind.*
> (Swami Gitananda)

The whole of the human community (the masses), maintain this territorial, animalistic mentality. What is puzzling is that any one individual actually has the possibility to rise above the divided, divisive way of living and being to the dimension where inner peace beckons, but hardly any one does.

Physically, the human organism is endowed with the essential hard wired equipment to access energetic unity. While the material functions of the body are routinely tampered with in the name of *medical science*, all techniques to enhance the more subtle features of human existence are overlooked. But within everyone is a *Center of Knowing*. Once The Guru releases its radiance, immediate and shocking recognition is aroused that is a piercing reminder of what has been forgotten (yet also what can be reclaimed). Seeing without the usual haze of internalized conditioning, even briefly, is indelibly imprinted in a resonant recess of the mind. In every life term, an intuitive detecting device resounds from the groove of remembrance whenever that pure vibration is perceived which explains the comfortable, yet mysterious familiarity inherent to the altered state from Marijuana.

> For those Blessed by the Marijuana Consciousness,
> There is an extraordinary palpable *knowing*
> That can be shared only among kindred travelers
> Whose *guide to reality* is rooted in the Holy Flower. (Bello)

The Center of Knowing is called *The Ajna Chakra*. It denotes a physical location in the human body as well as an energetic degree of refinement of the personality. When evolved, it is a *plateau of being* wherein the mind is still and perception clear. According to Yoga Science, *The Ajna Chakra* can be developed (or *opened*) with practice by the student, or by the intentional conveying of higher energies to the student from the Guru.

Ajna Chakra, located at the Center of the Eyebrows, is known as the *Third Eye* which refers to a way of *perceiving* that reflects a fuller, more highly developed comprehension than objective knowledge. It is subjective seeing in-tu-it that occurs during introspection, i.e., when the *mind field* is stilled and the usually opposite modes of body and mind are united. In the Hindu understanding, *Ajna* is the Sixth Chakra of human progress. It represents apprehending the highest energetic vortex possible for an individual. Although, there is yet a more advanced rung of refinement, at the ultimate plexus (actually above the crown of the head), personalized identification is dissolved.
(Note: The Chakra Hierarchy is not covered in this presentation.)

The Ajna Chakra is completely unsuspected by our modern, materialistic medicine, whose motto is *seeing is believing*. Thus the inner world is ignored. Ajna is a subtle center of invisible energetic streaming located where the two opposing channels of the Autonomic Nervous System (ANS) of stimulation and relaxation meet and become one. This joining occurs above where the brain is divided, thus allowing for integration of the dualities of opposing experience whereby perception and perspective change from separateness to unison.

Of Interest: According to esoteric science, the especially clear insight from *The Ajna Chakra* is said to be related to the Pineal Gland and even modern-day science has acknowledged that this organ (seemingly without any essential function) has its own unique light sensitivity. Meanwhile, Yoga Science has always maintained that this puzzling gland is the instrument for seeing into the inner world, where the faculty of intuition reigns. Humans usually have atrophied pineal glands as they no longer make use of its purpose, being overly obsessed with the external material world.

Resolving The Opposites
Whether by effort, karma, herb, good fortune or birth, the energy is sufficiently refined [so that the *pattern of the breath* is unrestricted, the mind field is without movement (thought) and the body is relaxed], the unified perspective of the Third Eye becomes operational. There is neither division in thought or deed. That is, if we observe the world and our place in it from the locale of where the ***two*** *opposing energies become single* **(at the physical point where the ANS channels merge)**, we naturally **know** the connectivity of everything. The opposing ANS modes (excitement or rest) are merged together to be experienced as *resolution of the opposites* (no division).

The entire thrust behind the philosophy of Yoga is precisely to link these two energetic circuits of split modes of experience, allowing for an unbiased, egoless orientation of *no thought*. When completely successful, the practices of Yoga Science result in physical, psychological and spiritual unity which is permanent. (Part III) Likewise, the basic interface of Marijuana molecules with the body sparks both sides of the ANS at once, sensed as resolving the opposites of relaxation and alertness.

(Information regarding the experience of enervating both sides of the ANS simultaneously via The Marijuana Effect; its significance for body/mind health as well as growth toward the spirit is the thesis of: <u>The Benefits of Marijuana: Physical, Psychological and Spiritual</u> *(not covered herein).*

When *The Ajna Chakra* is fully energized,
There is No Fear.
The individual resides in a *state of knowing*
All manifestation is known as an emanation of the One.

The ultimate goal of Yoga is psycho-physical merging with this highest possible vibration for an earthling where the inbuilt energy is fully efficient and the livingness/spirit/soul is free. That is, No extraneous dissonance intrudes. Such a rare evolution depicts an ascended perspective/perception, such as demonstrated in *Buddha-hood* or *Christ-Consciousness* where the person receives and integrates the entire extent of the radiance of the universe. It is a state unsullied by self-concern, with total release of body tension.

Purification practices to ready the student for such a power-filled reception/integration of the personality are integral to Yoga Science (especially *Kriya and Kundalini Yoga*). Then the untapped power of the seeker is released and the mistaken identification of a separate self *dissolves*. As noted, there is yet a further energetic ascent that is possible. Pure Energy resides at the Crown Chakra above the brain. This is the permanent state of *Enlightenment* where registration of the merging of the opposites is no longer personally experienced. **It just is.**

Psychologically, Higher Consciousness is rooted in the *Archetype* of human potential. It is inescapable yearning that we all have, usually misread and misdirected into worldly pursuits. *The Marijuana Consciousness* can be a blessed homing device which guides the focus to the inner abiding reality and away from transitory diversions. Of course, from the standpoint of human existence on the planet, growth toward the spirit is an unnecessary aspiration. In fact, people can easily maintain their whole lives throughout the commonly allotted number of years, without ever having suspected the higher planes of *living and being,* as most do.

Whether or not the influx of Cannabis into our primitive culture is in answer to the sorely felt need of the whole world for a change toward peace and harmony, or it is just a cyclical episode of the universe, or possibly, even just the march of science, the fact is: *Marijuana is very much with us at this time*, more so than at any other period in recent history. It is a household word. Its infusion into the society was first driven by the undercurrent, the fringes and the youth of the world, but now has gathered steam from mainstream-minded people who demand its health benefits. The point is, Marijuana is here to stay and it is only logical to assume that its restorative and energizing qualities will result in, not just healing of bodily disease but of the collective mind as well.

Compatible Gift of Marijuana

In the process of embracing the advanced consciousness that awaits us via increased energetic assimilation/integration by the lessons built-in to The Marijuana Consciousness, it is possible to access the road to a mentality beyond what is the normal existence of our specie. The fact that this ancient Plant Teacher preceded our specie by at least a hundred million years is significant. Whatever is most efficient for life is preserved and conserved in keeping with Natural Law. The human species is part of the process. We are the end product of various stages of evolution that were perfected before us.

The Cannabinoid System, requisite to balancing intricate cellular activity and generally enhancing the functioning of our whole being, including possibly obtaining entrance into super-consciousness, has been transmitted to our specie in convoluted stages throughout eons of time. We are after all products of that same soup of gestating aquatic life that preceded us. Retracing our heritage ultimately leads us back to our undeniable and co-evolving, shared origin with the Cannabis Sativa Plant.

Marijuana revitalizes The Cannabinoid System. It restores balance naturally through a primordial connection that cannot be denied. It communicates its own cosmic vitality to those organisms capable of integrating its ultra-refined vibration. But from the limited perspective of objective science, evidence of this harmonious and beneficial coalescence between this sacred Plant and the human species *has yet to be realized.* But contrasted to the dimness of our current one dimensional science, there is the clear and humble appreciation of what we arrogantly consider primitive mythology: when the Sativa was revealed as a *body-built* blessing from a Higher Source. Indeed, unquestionable facts from modern research; the experience of millions of people, everywhere; as well as the prehistoric *Legend of Mahadeva* are undeniably conjoined in the intuitive recognition and material confirmation of the compatibility of the *body-built* gift of Marijuana with our very being.

Religion vs. The Marijuana Consciousness

The wonder and devotion that The Marijuana Consciousness engenders have always been resisted by the controlling groups. While it is true that in India, Bhang was integrated into ceremonial worship, at the same time, independent employment of Bhang was discouraged. The privileged head honchos prescribed the accepted agenda, insuring that seekers were led along a path (however convoluted) that posed no threat to their rule.

In all epochs, enemies to *The Marijuana Consciousness* have argued that the advanced state experienced with Marijuana has no value since it is **not permanent** or earned through hard lessons and arduous training as proposed by self Proclaimed Guides. <u>But common sense makes it stunningly clear that raising awareness, if only momentarily, has an intrinsic, enduring significance which forever changes the person, regardless that the experience may not be maintained.</u>

Contrary to the view that lasting Enlightenment alone matters, in fact, every purposeful ascending toward the summit is first envisioned or seen from a lower level. To be sure, where and what one seeks are necessary perceptions for any climb that is to be chosen, especially the aspiration to spiritual unfoldment. In addition, according to esoteric teaching, the ascent to pure consciousness for each individual soul entails personal growth in awareness, perhaps even over the course of many lifeterms.

Every Moment of Awareness Matters.
Glimpses from Below of the Radiance Above
Serve as Strength to Continue on the Trek.
The Marijuana Experience is a Foretaste of Higher Realities.
It Bequeaths the Power to Persevere
On the Path to Enlightenment. (Bello)

Adam Kadmon – (Kabbalah Man)

The counterpart of perfect, permanent awareness in the lore of Jewish Mysticism is *Kabbalah Man*: an entity of Undivided Consciousness who has ascended to peak understanding by a series of awakened moments that have nothing to do with one another *until they touch*. That is, every conscious moment is a necessary piece of the puzzle in the mysterious journey to the destiny toward which each soul must travel for the ultimate super-conscious state to be realized. This principle recognizes that consciousness has physicality, and instances of unsullied perception are never wasted. Therefore, every soul traveler builds up a bank of mindful moments, separated by time and space that by design will automatically fuse together to unify the personality once a sufficient but undetermined garland of single such experiences accrues to form *Kabbalah Man* of the highest wisdom. This is envisioned as a process of constantly upgrading to the next dimension of knowing until there is the final Quantum Leap to evolutionary completion. According to this teaching, after many centuries or years or lifetimes or lessons, these moments merge together in radiance.

Objective Witness

In the esoteric teachings of Gurdjieff, known for its integration of truths from many spiritual traditions, the *Objective Witness* describes the *state of being* beyond the usual dualistic mode of human life. It is the *Center of Observation*, a built-in, although usually underdeveloped and energetically superior potential of our nature wherein perceptions are not muddied by desire. Acting and thinking for self interest is non-existent since there is no input from the personal ego. *The Yoga of Marijuana* summons this advanced viewpoint which is a psychological construct physically manifest at the The Third Eye, wherein dualism dissolves into a unified way of observing the world. This sixth evolutionary stage (*Ajna Chakra*) is beyond usual knowing, i.e., *The Intuitive Level.*

Identification Dissolves with Marijuana

The competitive materialism of accumulating more and better for oneself and everything attached to that identification, such as *my* children, *my* husband, *my* heritage, even *my* ideas is buoyed by the society as indicative of healthy individualism. Unfortunately, the consequence of fostering this separatist attitude from earliest childhood has quite naturally produced a world population continuously *on-guard* with a generally accepted mind-set against *the other*. And most unfortunately, this is now and has always been the signature of civilization. This is, directly opposed to the trust and compassion of what religion preaches; the effects of *The Marijuana Consciousness*; and the objectives of Yoga Science. It is also the reason why the government openly admitted its resistance to Marijuana during the Vietnam War since it found that soldiers were less aggressive under its influence. While patriotism is painted as love and loyalty to one country, the oppositional corollary is not addressed. Allegiance to one nation, comes only at the expense of fear and distrust of all other nations, which is the emotion necessary to maintain war.

Materialism Does Not Satisfy The Spirit.
It Ignores It!

Humans have an intrinsic curiosity into the invisible underlay. But this questioning quality is easily dulled by desire. Cultural goals are *getting ahead, getting a good life, wife, job* and *insurance plan*. Only marginally, if at all, is there interest in *giving, helping, serving, caring or loving* anyone outside one's sphere. Yet in the hypocrisy of our upbringing, these higher values are verbally prized but hardly practiced. Immediacy and Excess are paraded as answers to life by a lost generation and straight away sought by the next. But nothing unsubstantial can fill the basic thirst for truth. Institutional religion with its seemly platitudes offers no solace. It has no valid connection to *the legacy of experiential awe which stills the mind field and reflects the soul*. In fact, all roads to autonomous, life-enhancing practices have been condemned long ago (with malice and forethought) by the paternalism of *Church fathers* to *Founding fathers* and including the Father Figures of Heads of State, of Family, and as well internalized *into our Own Heads*. But what is forbidden is forever enticing. With today's instantaneous communication, the strong authoritarian resistance to the expanded awareness of Marijuana has ironically fueled it from being secreted to barefaced praise. Marijuana followers are drawn to the realism it engenders in direct correlation to the hollowness of the culture.

Present Potential for Growth is Magnified Today

Ironically but with absolute predictability, as the basic human need for meaning is disregarded; a painful spiritual abyss is eroding the foundation of materialism. Guidance concerning that which is immaterial, essential and non-transitory has been mislaid among diversion and trivia, which according to *The Teaching* is expected during periods of lost virtue, such as now in Kali Yuga. But it is no longer a hidden problem.

Luckily an equalizing principle to the present emptiness assures us that sincere efforts toward self-growth carry much more weight in Kali Yuga than in *Eras of Righteousness*. The Law of Scarcity holds true even in the realm of the spirit. When virtue is practically non-existent, it carries more weight than when it is abundant. In order to make headway beyond the usual or to climb the ladder toward higher consciousness, there must be a pit out from which one ascends. In this case, when there is little interest or determination or recognition of what is a clearer perspective of life in general, a little bit of awareness goes a long way. Today there are countless seekers brought to the threshold of the next evolutionary ascent by the blessing, kindness and wisdom of The Ancient Sativa. It serves as *The Accelerator* (Brown) for the Quantum Leap needed to rediscover our birthright of being fully conscious.

It seems a sardonic playwright has pierced the collective technological idolatry of a race gone empty. In the Third Act, the only possibility to save the players is a **denigrated flower.**

Regrettably, the watered down version of Yoga is very easily incorporated into this disruptive society, specifically because it cannot fulfill its promise of spiritual progress, without help. As acknowledged, few Yoga students attain real wisdom regardless of any expertise in posturing; just as the number of regular Marijuana partakers is far greater than those actually working toward self-growth. This just underscores the fact that most people, whether regular *tokers* or skillful learners of fitness remain *asleep,* kept in check by a mechanical process of self-interest for material gain.

> *In Kali Yuga, Wealth alone will be the deciding factor of Nobility*
> *Instead of Righteous Behavior or Merit.*
> *Brute Force will be the only Standard*
> *Establishing or Deciding what is Righteous or Just.*
> (Bhagavata Purana, XII, 2:2-3)

Imbalance Maintains The Culture

In the divided world of the empowered and the enslaved, controlling the population is sustained by diversion and division. Thrills and disappointments costumed in importance produce a bi-polar population of delusion and confusion. Interests outside the *busy box* of continuous striving are considered *deviant*. Long denied reflective tendencies that are re-awakened by psycho-physical balance, as occurs with the *liberated pattern of the breath* accompanied by *silence of the mind*, are directly opposed to competition and consumerism. An imbalanced, unhealthy citizenry produces the greatest profit. Rushing, striving, grasping without time to relax or breathe is the modus operandi that maintains the wheels of commerce. But though little interest and almost no time are allotted to the invisible dimension that defines human life, in the eternal battle of forces, there exists the unmistakable backdrop of balance. Ironically, by denying the spirit, the materialistic void has intensified the felt-need to embrace what is real.

Who is Interested and Why is Undecipherable

For every serious student who seeks self-knowledge, some realization along the life path at some receptive and possibly predestined moment revealed an insight that sparked the quest. Receptivity of that individual just happened to be at the junction of the universe that teases out the clarity to begin the trip away from worldly values. It is one of those *inexplicables*. Maybe it was accidental or maybe it was fate. Perhaps the seeker's *essence/ livingness/ soul* or *spirit* reached the refinement that appreciates the *significance of it all* (the esoteric position). Whatever begins the intention to search beyond the surface of existence cannot be deciphered. But at some stage of life, or for certain people in general, or for as long as one recalls, introspection and *time out* were/are life necessities. The companionship of Marijuana in such a scenario can be said to serve as *Arouser, Guide, Intensifier, Humiliator* and *Comforter*, oftentimes in that order.

> *Marijuana Consciousness… ever so gently, shifts the center of attention from habitual shallow, verbal guidelines and repetitive secondhand ideological interpretations of experience to more direct, slower, absorbing, occasionally microscopically minute engagement with sensing phenomena.* (Allen Ginsberg)

With *The Marijuana Consciousness*, one-dimensional concerns dwindle. There is a gradual turning to inner interests, taking energy from the external with less credence and allegiance to outside forces and bosses. Hearing a *Higher Calling;* sensing a *Grander Scheme;* seeing the cultural cruelty; signal rebellion while the tolerance of *The Marijuana Consciousness* imperils the competitive foundation of the society. It denounces private nationalized selfishness and lends a clear promise to the next step in evolution. Marijuana lends hope to the possibility of a spiritual (R)evolution in the midst of secular life.

The Inner Human Make-Up Prevails
As It once Was, So It May Be Becoming Again
Today, the world of Men and Women has lost its way; but there is legend that it was not always so. Ancient recordings, archetypal intuitions and historical artifacts all reveal that essential humane qualities of kindness and mercy, as well as curiosity in deep cosmological truth did co-exist in thriving communities which suggest that it can be again as it once was. The increasing draw to this Holy Earth Medicine is one such harbinger that a homecoming to wonder and awe may be at hand. *The River of Conscious Intent* is flowing determinately, impelled by inborn longing for the lost path back to the real. This undeniable impulse has coalesced into a bridge between ancient wisdom and modern science, including practicable applications of yoga meditation, acupuncture, aromatherapy, reflexology, massage, now all verified by modern technology. The age-old skills are being ushered into diverse areas of contemporary life escorted by the expanded awareness gifted to old and young alike by Cannabis Sativa.

*(Personally, my own **Guru**, nearly 50 years ago charged me with the task of helping to fashion this bridge about which I feel humbly grateful for being granted the opportunity to accomplish this via my work with Marijuana and Consciousness)*

Materialism Giving Birth to Spiritual Resurgence

The *youth* with their inclusive and rebellious orientation have embraced Marijuana. They realize its contribution to noble, global ideals and welcome its liberating effects. In addition, the *principles* of *justice and freedom for all* have prompted *middle-aged liberals* to object to prohibiting such a healthful and harmless plant. Meanwhile, *patients* and **elderly citizens** comprise a coalition demanding Marijuana Medicine for relief of suffering and/or discomfort. **Scattered among these diverse groups, is the recurrent streaming of those of us whose allegiance to the Primordial Sativa is not based on principles of justice or medical need or belief, but is simply the upshot of being imbued with the Magic of Marijuana.**

From Pantheism to Hinduism;
From the Buddhists, Zoroastrians, Esssenes;
The Jewish, Christian, Moslem, Sufi, Theraputae of Egypt,
To the Bantus, Zulas, Hottentots etc., of Africa;
All used Cannabis/Hemp for fiber, food, oil, medicine,
And (one of) Their Sacred Religious Catalysts. (Herer)

Eastern Understanding Reinvigorated

The reality that human existence can be more than momentary pleasure is catapulting a collective spontaneous return to long held global traditions that venerated The Plant of Peace for its mind expansion properties along with a welcomed sense of belonging to grandness. Nonetheless, despite historical and scientific substantiation that spiritual seekers always utilized *plant teachers (and still do)*, Institutional Religions continue to oppose independent spiritual endeavors. To ensure their own positions, they simply deny the truth!

India Does Not Deny Its Heritage

Thankfully, the Indian culture, with its impressive intact records of 10,000+ years does not and realistically speaking, cannot credibly deny its enduring *legacy from Cannabis Sativa*. It was woven into the very fabric of daily life, acclaimed in the hallowed ancient scripture, necessary for its myriad, mystical ceremonies and gratefully venerated for the consciousness it imparts. It was employed consistently for its therapeutic and healing benefits for thousands of years. Predictably, as we have seen, even then, The High Priests entrenched in their positions of control, were themselves guilty of trying to co-opt the wonder of this natural Primordial Guru. (Part II)

From Whence Has Come This Wisdom

In the Era of the *Glory of India*, there was a spiritual awareness that appears to have been built into the entire society. The unswerving determination of the Indian ethic to delve into universal mysteries was not spawned by desire for power or even for possessions. The distinction of a culture actually integrating its higher ideals into daily life is awarded to the India-of-old! Its collective emphasis was upon experiential realization of the Divine. Bhang was an integral, instigating and essential component. Pursuit of such a lofty goal was fostered by both practicality and Providence. With the encouragement of the culture; inspired always by the gentle Sativa built into daily routines; served by comfort, leisure and security, the introspection, motivation and methods for attending to timeless values and eternal questions flourished. No other civilization can lay claim to such a spiritual legacy.

> *The Infinite (presents)... In an infinite variety of aspects*
> *Spirituality is the Master Key of the Indian Mind.*
> *It is the Dominant Inclination of India*
> *It has grown out of her Inborn Spiritual Tendency.*
> *Her religion is a natural out flowering.*
> (Sri Aurobindo)

The Depth of Indian Philosophy

As noted, Indian scripture verifies cultures millions of years ago, accessed from deep meditation that reflects and supports the reality of infinite recurrence. While The West dates sacred texts of India from 2000 to 10000 BC, The East, oriented to the cycles of Yugas upholds **The Eternal Way**, (*Sanātana Dharma*) that is universal for all peoples; billions of years old; identical to the *Science of Vibration*; and manifest incalculable times over. To explain *eternal* law, an example given is *gravity*, in existence regardless of its discovery. Likewise, truth exists regardless of recognition. Today there is little interest and less knowledge in the unseen underlay. Nevertheless it exists.

The Universal Realism of Indian Philosophy

The *Vedas* is considered *revealed* eternal truth. As the oldest sacred text of this world, it is the undisputed authority for (almost all) Indian Thought. *Revelation* is encountered in pure meditation in the dimension of *undifferentiated consciousness* through a mysterious grace that cannot be summoned. It is usually exposed during enlightened eras by highly evolved individuals, oftentimes termed *avatars, saints, prophets, gods* or in current vernacular, *geniuses* who exhibit superior abilities. Besides *revelation*, Tradition honors wisdom *that is re-collected,* such as ancient legends and customs of virtuous peoples that simplifies or reflects the lessons of The Vedas.

Indian Esoteric Understanding

Homogeneous conditioning of the world society is now a fact. Instant communication has merged East with West. In swift, sure fashion, centuries' old taboos have been discarded. Ideals are defunct. In the midst of these broad transitions, one might conclude that the enduring Indian Philosophy has *had its day*. But the Indian wisdom knows that upheavals in history are but evidence of the everlasting law of the cycles of outer change, upheld unendingly by the ground of the Eternal.

Regardless the acculturating similarities, there is no doubt that the Indian sophistication is far different from the narrow perspective of materialism. Western indoctrination does not enlist or even envision a sense of purpose beyond the individual ego because (as a newly formed civilization, relatively speaking,) it has not yet reached the necessary plateau of comprehension borne of *cultural time*. In contrast, the mature, long enduring patience of a society that is tens of thousands of years in the making does not grasp the extent of short-sightedness of an undeveloped mindset. The Marijuana Consciousness offsets this inequality through the unfamiliar but welcomed event of fullness to/of/in the present moment whereby the conditioning of shallowness dissolves.

In The Vedas, clarity from *The Sativa* is both *revealed* and *remembered knowledge*. Marijuana is acknowledged constantly in the Indian scripture, its virtues extolled for its joy, comfort, wisdom and loyalty. Although its legacy is recounted in Indian Lore of thousands of years past, yet its beguiling beneficial effects still endure in perfect sync with modern life.

> *This Book is Memory of Embedded Experience,*
> *Eminently Supported by* The Vedas.
> *The Yoga of Marijuana Remains in the Subconscious Realm*
> *Yet is Ever Present.* (Bello)

Religion grows in India as wild flowers in the forest. (Ellis)

> *What is meant by religion in the Indian sense is far different from the faith-based non-scientific jargon of Western religions. Unlike other Religions: The Hindu Religion Does not Claim any One Prophet, Worship any One God, Believe in any One Philosophic Concept, Follow any One Religious Rite. It Does not Satisfy Traditional Features of Religion or Creed. It is a Way of Life and Nothing More.*
> (Supreme Court of India)

India of Old

The bounteous resources of early India, protected by sea and mountains, enjoyed an exceptionally hospitable setting that encouraged occasion for majestic art, enchanting music, scholarly literature and science, as well as fundamental ethical values and deep curiosity for spiritual matters. This was a peaceful land, attuned to contemplative, creative tolerance. Its efficient, compassionate society quite effortlessly gravitated to the higher ideals while partaking of Holy Bhang as part of its worship; for recreation; as an aid for inner growth; as a healthful and healing tonic and as a versatile medicine.

This philosophy that generated cooperation amid its citizens was born from sincere interest in the farthest possibilities for human evolution. Rather than replacing one understanding with another, Indian Thought has been layered century upon century according to integrative principles and harmonious practices conducive to accessing the enigma of existence. The countless impressions (cultural, political, physical, social, environmental and spiritual) impinging upon the mentality of so vast and varied a populace as India were incorporated across many levels of comprehension, at once, and over the course of thousands of years, during which time, the entire society was constantly infused with the refined awareness imparted from the ever present Cannabis Sativa.

Yoga: Hidden Roots and Modern Relevance

Yoga Science was kept hidden simply because it could not be appreciated by the masses. To interpret the empirical science of Yoga with the capacity to implement its potential calls for a mature intuitive faculty and the rare student with one-pointed steadfast discipline. Actually, *The Teaching* was also concealed for millennia to protect It. *Yoga is most secret and not to be divulged indiscriminately. It should be told only to those positively qualified to receive it. It weakens when it becomes known to all.*
  (Siva Samhita, Chapter V)

Yoga is not a pastime for the main community, either now or in the past. Although ancient India was based in spiritual values with loyal supporters, nevertheless the most arduous skills to unlock the ultimate treasure of enlightenment were guarded like gold, revealed only to worthy aspirants. As it was then, so it is now. Most people are not concerned with refining their vibration or whether or not there is more to life than personal gain. While there has been a major influx of Eastern knowledge to the Western, its depth escapes the superficial mind. For the masses, Yoga is but a communal exercise routine with few participants ever suspecting any of the essential reasons for practice.

The secrets of Yoga were discovered without technology by determined and inspired sages who plumbed the depths of their own beings. Methods for transforming a human life from ordinary self-concern to the unified consciousness of *liberation from fear* were sought and found in deep meditation by direct vision (Darsana). According to the teaching, Yogic Masters studied over untold numbers of lifetimes, always imbued with enhanced awareness of energetic refinement from Marijuana, or its promise, or its past experience, or its memory or the assurance of what had been revealed by it.

The Marijuana Consciousness and the inner knowledge gleaned from Yoga Practice are similarly indescribable states of being. While the *Science of Yoga* is an outgrowth of the Indian world, the *originating influence* of the omnipresent Sativa must never be forgotten. It was the energetic matrix within which the depth of wisdom and the pinnacle of inspiration were born.

Yoga Science is the Map to our Hidden Potentials.
The Marijuana Consciousness visits those Potentials.
The Science of Yoga and The Marijuana Consciousness
Are Married in their Parallel Results
And By their Primeval Linked Past. (Bello)

Yoga of Marijuana vs. Classical Yoga

The Marijuana Consciousness can be likened to stepping
purposefully onto the Penthouse terrace all day long,
Perhaps for most of the days of one's life,
So that the imprinting from the Glorious Sky
Becomes, what was described by my Guru, Swami Rama as:
A *Good Habit that Dissolves Disharmony - which is* **Unity.**
(Bello)

Only Unconsciousness would keep such a gift from the people.
(Lord Siva, *Bestower of Deliverance upon All Beings*)

In contrast, *Yoga Science* is akin to perceiving the world
Through an obstructed Skylight
With the Intentional practice of purifying one's Vision
By increasingly more tedious but guaranteed discipline
So that one will automatically
Merge with the Glorious All-encompassing Unity.

SUMMING UP

The *practice of calming the mind* is a continuous and deliberate exercise toward de-escalation of the imaginary mental clutter of desires, fears, memories and delusions that fill our heads and waste our energy. We are ever Un-Present to What IS. Yoga Science is the practice of noticing rather than judging (what anything and everything means or where it is from or whether or not it is good or bad for oneself). Advancing to the goal usually takes place in a hierarchical fashion, so that the student becomes more aware, less distracted and therefore more energized over time. At some point in the march back to truth, there is immediate and brilliant insight into the reality, thus the term *self-realization.*

This knowledge from India has coalesced into a subjective hands-on scientific teaching valid for every person in every situation. Yoga offers a comprehensive life-long way of living and being since working toward its ideals is the beginning of growth toward the spirit. Realizations uncovered, practiced, venerated and passed down were always in conjunction with the ever-present majestic Cannabis Sativa. Scandalous as the evidence may be concerning both the formal interpretation and the modern instruction of Patanjali's Classical Yoga: the accounts from history; both ancient and contemporary science; deductive and inductive logic; respected testimonials; as well as the personal experience of multitudes are all features that point to the unmentionable yet unquestionable fact that:

Yoga is the Child of The Marijuana Consciousness.

According to The Teaching,
The Bliss of Enlightenment is the Natural Birthright of Us All
If we just Pay Attention.

Yoga is The Practice of Paying Strict Attention.

The Marijuana Experience is an Invitation to Attentiveness.
The Yoga of Marijuana Invokes and Summons Awareness.
It is the catalyst
By which the rewards of Mindfulness are Realized.
(Bello)

END OF PART I - <u>The Yoga of Marijuana</u>

AUTHOR'S AFTERWORD

Part I

The preceding work represents the general philosophical and historical underpinnings behind both Classical Yoga and the *Yoga of Marijuana*. The sociological structure as it unfolds predictably within the cosmology of the times is offered as the reason for the heart and soul *felt-need* of some members of the Human Race for The Marijuana Consciousness. In addition, the unbroken ancient tradition of *The Yoga of Marijuana* as it re-asserts itself on the world scene and its undeniable, yet hidden kinship with Yoga Science are revealed for those ready to resume their evolutionary voyage from some prior time, state and/or embodiment.

Part II

<u>The Tantra of Marijuana</u> will present the origin and profound philosophy of the supremely misunderstood Tantric Path as it evolved from the primeval purity of the aboriginal mind. While the comprehensive tolerance and refined practices of Eastern Thought are progressive, profound and far reaching, Tantra is unquestionably the crowning pinnacle of its legacy. Interestingly enough, this prehistoric teaching is considered the most suitable Path to Enlightenment for the distracted mind of the present era, while Shiva, Lord of Bhang fits into the mix as the symbol of conscious pulsation of the universe, in keeping with the most advanced contemporary science.

> *The Dance of Shiva is the Dancing Universe,*
> *The ceaseless flow of energy going through*
> *An infinite variety of patterns*
> *That melt into one another.*
> (Capra)

Hinduism is the only religion that propounds
...Life Cycles of the Universe
... And Infinite Number of Deaths and Rebirths.

As in Modern Physics,
Hindu Cosmology envisaged the Universe having a Cyclical Nature.
The end of each Kalpa (period) brought about by Shiva's Dance
Is the Beginning of the Next.

Rebirth follows Destruction.
(Carl Sagan)

Part III

<u>Marijuana and Yoga Practice</u> is the integration *of* specific Yogic training with the underlying principle behind each practice for health and heightened awareness, mirrored in and originating from the subtle **Benefits of Marijuana.**

APPENDIX

Reincarnation and *Recurrence (Rebirth)*

The following explanation addresses the topics of *Recurrence* and *Reincarnation* and the distinction between the two as taught to me by my Guru Swami Rama of the Himalayas and including the viewpoint of Gurdjieff, a known teacher of the integration of various, ancient esoteric knowledge. It is not the formatory explanation one finds in texts that are diluted for the modern Western mind which speaks of ghosts and being able to communicate with some mysterious *other side*. Also please note that I am just transferring the teaching as it was taught to me. I have no such knowledge of the subject other than as one who studied under those who claim *to know*; in the case of Swami Rama, I would add that he appeared in all manner and form to be a Tantric Yoga Master, as he stated. I am presenting these many years of Eastern Studies to the reader as non-experiential lessons and nothing more.

The wisdom of Yoga Science recognizes the uniqueness of every person; the individualized plateaus upon which each lifetime is situated and that every exclusive setting serves the seeker in unfoldment to spiritual realization. This is not by Divine Intervention but simply the natural consequence of cause and effect (Karma). And further, this has nothing to do with punishment or reward doled out by a paternalistic Super Being as in many religious disciplines. Instead Karma is more like a record with grooves that imprint certain vibrations in the unconscious experience that travels with the energetic containment (*soul*) through many embodied life-terms and which become expressed behaviors or repressed traits that are played repeatedly and very mechanically until the manifested personality takes charge of these long-standing entrenched ruts with the conscious intention to let silence/stillness reign. The aim is to smooth out the vibrational impressions by whatever means available. Then one is free from the Law of Karma and the Cycle of Recurrence (Rebirth).

Timeless revelations of The Doctrine of Reincarnation and the science that upholds The Principle of Recurrence, called the *Wheel of Life* in Buddhism, have predictably been dismissed by the contemporary world view which is focused exclusively on the physical plane, thereby guaranteeing that the mainstream majority remains ignorant of the (higher) potential inherent in human nature. We have seen that awakening to these hidden realms of being is part and parcel of *The Marijuana Consciousness* and at the same time is abhorrent to materialism. While the major culture moves along the horizontal surface of existence, there are those who are choicelessly sparked to search out the Deeper Mystery in response to the indelibly imprinted prior experience of the trek to Self-Realization or Liberation.

In order to understand the difference between Reincarnation and Recurrence, Universal Laws of physics and consciousness apply. Reincarnation naturally is the wish of every mortal. In the normal human state of *fear of death*, never dying is utterly preferable. But the ending of the personality is inevitable.

**Whatever is Born, Dies.
Only the U*ncreated* Remains.**

Physical law states that everything falls back to its origin (entropy). The galaxy will one day return to the dense force of a Black Hole. But the energetic matrix that expands into physical manifestation (*Arc of Descent*) is never destroyed. So it is in the death of the organism. The enlivening factor simply transits to some other state. **It Recurs**. Thus is the continuous Rebirth of unconscious life. Science teaches that our cosmos will one day disappear only to recur again out from the Black Hole of the densest energy, (*Bindu*, in Eastern Metaphysics) from which it unfurls endlessly. So it is with the encapsulated energy (soul) that continues to assume a different form with no knowledge of prior experiences until it awakens to its true nature as simply a part of the universal life force.

According to the Law of Recurrence, the *livingness* or *soul* of every person (*permanent individuality*) and its mental faculty are irrevocably although unconsciously bonded. In death, the individual history is lost along with the *transitory personality which is formed anew with every incarnation* yet the vibrational containment continues or *recurs*, albeit without memory of prior births. This simply means that the identified person, that which we call "me" dies along with the body. The person as he or she knows itself ends at death. What remains is the energy and the grooves of experience about which every normal person is ignorant. When the energy departs the body, it changes form or remains in an energetic state. It is not destroyed. Life-term after life-term, along the course of human bondage, the contained energy, what can be called *the soul* but without the usual religious connotation, is reborn into varied experiences. <u>Finally after eons of life lessons, and only when the aspect of consciousness intervenes **It Realizes Itself** as a radiant flash of the *Over-Soul*.</u>

Of course, the *goal for the soul* is to escape from the cycle of involuntary, unconscious Recurrence which can only take place with a silent mind so that there is a clear perception of what is happening and what can be accomplished. That is, when the energetic sheath is refined completely so that mental noise is non-existent **OR** when the soul is disrobed from its baggage of identification with the insatiable desires of the myriad personalities, then there is freedom from the dense emotions of possessiveness, which is defined as Liberation from the Wheel of Life and Death. According to Rajmani:

> *When in the course of its journey...The Life Force*
> *Associates itself with matter, matter becomes animate – Birth*
> *When the Life Force disassociates itself from matter,*
> *Matter becomes inert – Death.*
> *...The Life Force coming into manifestation and returning to its*
> *Un-manifest state is the anatomy of Birth and Death*

According to the thesis, Reincarnation is completely different from Recurrence, yet it is absolutely connected.

> *Rebirth and Reincarnation are a continuum,*
> *Not two completely separate phenomena.*
> *Every Reincarnation began with Rebirth.*
> *Each Rebirth is an opportunity to move forward*
> *On the ladder of our personal evolution.* (Rajmani)

Reincarnation is an extremely rare, mysterious event wherein a conscious soul willfully is embodied on the physical plane. Of course, there is a huge gap between understanding this possibility on an intellectual basis and being able to integrate its meaning with our modern materialistic mindset. Yet it fits with all the archetypal intuitions that many developed beings have surmised throughout the history of humanity; it is in total accord with the concepts and provings that are taking place in Quantum Physics; and it is taught as unconditional truth in The Yogic Tradition:

> *Such an extraordinary individual is able to descend only because they once ascended…Seeing the body and senses falling into the grip of old age and disease, realizing that these tools no longer served any purpose, they willfully and happily left them behind. This is called ascending instead of dying helplessly. Such extraordinary people thus have the privilege of Descending. When they reincarnate, Their knowledge and experience return with them.* (Rajmani)

Such an *Avatar* reincarnates when the time is deemed right for those receptive and primed to appreciate the significance of transcendence. To Reincarnate or to *take a body* (as the saying goes) defines the state of full integration of the spiritual force of a realized soul with total recall of all past embodiments.

> *Reincarnation is a rare Privilege.*
> *It commands respect and carries an Aura of Glory.* (Rajmani)

But for the average or ordinary personality, *Recurrence* is the usual course of events. There is no knowledge whatsoever of past births. Although, infrequently there are breakthroughs from the subconscious realm into the conscious mind from some distant past life for certain people, such as in hypnosis or when there is a shock to the system, nevertheless, these happenings are just snippets of memories that seep into awareness without willfulness and in no way resemble what is meant by the Mystery of Reincarnation. *Reincarnation* is often mistakenly used in the vernacular to imagine restoration of the personality but nothing can fulfill such a hope which is born of the basic human fear of death.

The preceding explanation is one-dimensional. I can in no way do justice to the profoundly detailed cosmological science of The Eastern Philosophy which expounds with unimaginable precision the transference of energy into matter, and includes *The Theory of Recurrence of the Soul* which fits perfectly with the modern *provings* of Quantum Physics.

A simple analogy of a hand in a glove may help to clarify the Mystery. Let us hypothesize that every finger in a glove is only as aware as the average person. Therefore every finger is separated within its own ideas and personality (the *sheath* of conditioning) with no knowledge of anything except through its own gloved (*veiled*) sight. It is ignorant of the hand to which it belongs and of which it is an intrinsic part. Its vision is obscured by the fabric of its thinking. It does not imagine the arm to which the hand is connected, although all the flesh and bones of both hand and arm are of the identical substance. It is very busy with its own hopes, dreams, plans and fears. The separated entity is literally in the darkness of its own delusions. It never steps outside itself. It does know, however that it will die. It is afraid and self-concerned. It comforts itself by having or imagining having more than other fingers. Finally, in fear, it dies off, never realizing its true make-up.

But the energy that enlivened it continues. It takes on the covering of yet another finger, indefinitely. Over a long time, the glove begins to wear thin and perhaps one of the fingers is able to surmise more to its existence. It intuits that to which it is inherently connected. As that particular finger works through the materia of the cloth that keeps it from seeing the truth, more and more light falls upon it so that there is greater and greater suspicion and curiosity to understand its origin and its connectivity to the rest of all that exists. We can say it develops a Higher Consciousness than is the norm. Something triggers that semi-knowledge. In passing through its life-term, there has been a bestowing of clear sight. Such an enlightening may come through many forms. It is called *Guru* in Indian Philosophy. Those on the Marijuana Path have found such a light in the ancient Sativa.

Sometimes by some inexplicable Grace, one finger reaches a plateau of understanding that is *extraordinary*. It *realizes itself as emanation of the Supreme Spiritual Energy*. This may be from sequential imprintings on the encapsulated Life Force as it travels through embodiments. But by whatever method such a blessing arises - in that dimension of Self Realization, the history of prior embodiments is apparent. That is what is meant by being able to look backward and forward into the illusion of time where there is the ability to see the myriad materializations of ITSELF. But until such an unfathomable awareness, the cycle of life and death continues. **It recurs**.

Regardless of the lost veneration of the spirit in this current period, the invitation to see for oneself is ever extended. While the outer life is relentlessly in flux, one can work toward the non-transitory realm of silence to which Yoga Science is geared and to which the Guru speaks. The symbolism of Indian cosmology of the unending rebirth and dissolution of the world is depicted as the continuous comings and goings of Shiva, God of The Universe, **Lord of Bhang (Marijuana)**.

BIBLIOGRAPHY

Adyashanti, The Way of Liberation: A Practical Guide to Spiritual Enlightenment, Open Gate Sangha, 2013

Aranya, Swami H.
Yoga Philosophy of Patanjali, Univ. of Calcutta, 1963

Aurobindo, Sri, Synthesis of Yoga, Lotus Press 1990

Ben Zion, Raphael, translated from Hebrew,
An Anthology of Jewish Mysticism, Judaica Press, Inc., 1981

Bennett, Chris, Cannabis and the Soma Solution, 2010, Trine Day

Blofeld, John, trans., The Zen Teaching of Huang Po, Grove Press, 1994

Brown, Jeff, Marijuana and the Bible, 2012, CreateSpace

Chang, Garma C. C., Teachings and Practice of Tibetan Tantra, University Books, 1963

Feuerstein, George & Wilbur, Ken
The Yoga Tradition: Its History, Literature, Philosophy and Practice, Hohm Press, 2001

Frawley & Lad, The Yoga of Herbs: An Ayurvedic Guide to Herbal Medicine, Lotus Press, 1986

Ganguli, Sri Kisari Mohan
The Path of Yoga from The Mahabharata, Santi Parva, Sections CCXXXIX and CCXL

Hanh, Thich Nhat, The Miracle of Mindfulness,
Beacon Press, 1999

Hoffman, Edward, The Way of Splendor: Jewish Mysticism and Modern Psychology, Shambhala, 1981
Institute of Medicine (IOM), *Marijuana and MEDICINE: Assessing the Science Base*, 1999

King, Francis, Tantra for Westerners, Destiny Books, 1986

Krishnamurti, Jiddu, The Flight of The Eagle,
Harper & Row, 1971

Lakshaman JEE, Swami, Kashmir Shaivism, The Secret Supreme, SUNY Press, Shaiva Trust, 1988

Leary, Timothy, The Politics of Ecstacy,
Ronin Publishing, 1998

Matics, Marion L., Entering the Path of Enlightenment,
The Macmillan Company, 1970

Menon, Ramesh, Bhagavata Purana, Rupa & Co., 2011

Ouspensky, P.D., The Psychology of Man's Possible Evolution, Vintage Books, 1950

Singh, Jaideve, (trans.), Siva Sutras: The Yoga of Supreme Identity, Indological Publ., India, 1979

Siva Samhita, Chapter V

Sivananda, Sri Swami, Thought Power,
Divine Life Society, 1996

Suzuki, Daisetz Teitaro, The Zen Doctrine of No Mind,
Christmas Humphreys, (edit.), Weiser 1991

Swami Rama, Book of Wisdom,
Himalayan Institute of Yoga Science, India, 1979

Taimini, I.K., The Science of Yoga, Quest Books, 1961;

Tigunait, Pandit Rajmani, Tantra Unveiled,
Himalayan Institute Press, 2007

Tigunait, Pandit Rajmani,
Seven Systems of Indian Philosophy,
The Himalayan International Institute, 1983

Vivekananda, Swami, Raja-Yoga,
Ramakrishna Vivekananda Centre of NY, 1982

Woodruff, Sir John,
Garland of Letters, Ganesh and Co., 6th Ed., 1974.

INDEX

A

Adam Kadmon
   (Kabbalah Man) · 68
Adam's Bridge · 53
Adyashanti · 13
Allen Ginsberg · 73
Amrita · 45
Anandamide · 61
Angiosperms · 59
Attentional Shifts · 40
Autonomic Nervous System · 36, 64

B

Benefits of Marijuana · 19, 45, 62, 83
Beyond the Mind · 31, 38, 48
Bhang · 45, 49, 51, 67, 75, 78
Bhangi · 32
Body Born · 45

C

Cannabinoid System · 59, 60, 61, 62, 66
Cannabis Sativa · 16, 17, 18, 51, 59, 60, 73, 75, 78, 81
Carl Sagan · 83
Center of Knowing · 35
Center of Observation · 69
Chakra, Ajna · 36, 65, 69
Chakra, Crown · 65
Chakras · 47, 65
Charles Tart · 40
Classical Yoga · 13, 30, 34, 81, 82
Cosmic Ocean · 45

D

Dr. Andrew Weil · 25
Dr. Ralph Mechoulem · 61
Dualism · 17, 63, 69
Dualistic · 37, 38, 39, 69
Dvapara Yuga · 52

E

Ellis · 77
Enculturation · 43
Endogenous · 61
Enlightenment · 13, 23, 33, 34, 42, 56, 65, 67, 68, 79, 81, 82
Exogenous · 60

F

Flower · 7, 17, 28, 35, 44, 62, 71
Fritjof Capra · 82

G

George Feuerstein · 30, 33, 34
Getting High · 42
Gurdjieff · 69, 85

H

Harappan · 52
Harappan society · 52
Hinduism · 74, 83
Huang Po · 39
Humiliator · 62, 72

I

India · 75, 76, 77, 78, 79, 81
Indian scripture · 54, 76, 77

Institute of Medicine · 62
Intentionality · 46

J

Jack Herer · 74
Jeff Brown · 34, 62
Joan Bello · 13, 16, 46

K

Kabbalah Man · 68
Kali Yuga · 52, 53, 70, 71
Karma · 64, 85
Krishnamurti · 39, 41

L

Living Master · 55
Lord of Bhang · 45, 82, 90

M

Magnetic Center · 47
Mahadeva · 45, 67
Mantra · 32, 33
Marijuana · 13, 16, 17, 18, 19, 20, 23, 25, 27, 28, 29, 30, 34, 35, 39, 40, 41, 42, 44, 45, 46, 49, 51, 57, 58, 60, 61, 62, 63, 64, 66, 67, 70, 71, 72, 73, 74, 77, 79, 81, 83
Marijuana and The Bible · 34, 62
Marijuana Consciousness · 15, 16, 18, 23, 25, 26, 29, 38, 39, 41, 42, 46, 49, 51, 57, 58, 63, 65, 66, 67, 69, 73, 77, 79, 80, 82, 86
Marijuana Effect · 15
Marijuana Experience · 17, 68
Marijuana Practice · 25
Marion Woodman · 43
Master Teacher · 55
Meditation · 32, 33, 34, 41, 42, 47, 48, 54, 55, 76, 79
Mind Field · 35, 36, 37, 38, 41, 46, 64, 70

N

No Thought · 38, 40, 47, 64

O

Objective Witness · 69
One-pointed · 78
Oshadhi · 21, 32, 33

P

Paranoia · 18, 62
Patanjali · 31, 38, 51, 81
Pattern of the Breath · 26, 42, 44, 58, 62, 64, 72
Pausing the Mind · 40
Pranayama · 42

R

Rajmani · 50, 87, 88
Recurrence · 31, 76, 85, 86, 87, 88, 89
Rig Veda · 54

S

Satya Yuga · 52
Science of Vibration · 76
Science of Yoga · 18, 31, 43, 78, 79
Self-identification · 43
Self-realization · 23, 31, 32, 38, 42, 48, 55, 58, 80, 86
Sense of Well-being · 26, 42, 44, 62
Shiva · 82
Silent Mind · 41, 87
Siva Samhita · 78
Spaces between Thoughts · 40, 44
Special Appreciation: · 6
Sri Aurobindo · 75
Sri Ramana Maharishi · 35
Supreme Court of India · 77
Swami Rama · 35, 80, 85

T

Taimini · 48, 49
THC receptor · 59
The Accelerator · 34, 71
The Breath · 26, 42, 43, 44, 46, 47, 58, 63
The Culture · 25, 27, 70, 75
The Guru · 34, 35, 90
The Marijuana Path · 20, 34, 90
The Pattern of the Breath · 43
The Tantra of Marijuana · 23, 32, 51, 82
The Third Eye · 36, 64, 65, 69

The Trilogy · 23
The Vedas · 45, 49, 51, 58, 76, 77
Thich Nhat Hanh · 43
Timothy Leary · 29
Treta Yuga · 52, 54

U

Unbroken Tradition · 18, 57
Undifferentiated Consciousness · 38, 76

W

Way of Herbs · 32

Y

Yoga · 30, 34, 36, 37, 38, 41, 42, 49, 50, 58, 64, 65, 71, 78, 79, 81
Yoga Master · 85
Yoga Meditation · 73
Yoga Movement · 30
Yoga of Herbs · 32, 33
Yoga of Marijuana · 57, 69, 77, 81, 82
Yoga Philosophy · 30
Yoga Science · 19, 23, 30, 31, 34, 36, 37, 38, 42, 52, 64, 65, 69, 78, 79, 80, 82, 85, 90
Yoga Sutras · 31
Yogic Masters · 79
Yuga · 52

Notes

attachment → faith
Depression — Gratitude

Made in the USA
Columbia, SC
28 September 2017